MASTERING STRESS

A LifeStyle Approach

David H. Barlow, Ph.D.

State University of New York at Albany

Ronald M. Rapee, Ph.D.

University of Queensland - Australia

AMERICAN HEALTH
Publishing Company

Library of Congress

ISBN 1-878-513-05-2

Address orders to:

The LEARN® Education Center
1555 W. Mockingbird Lane, Suite 203
Dallas, Texas 75235

In Dallas (214) 637-7700
Or Toll Free (800) 736-7323
Fax Number (214) 637-0529

Acknowledgements

Special thanks to Leslie Telfer for her substantial contribution to this book.

Permission to reprint cartoons was granted by the Universal Press Syndicate, Tribune Media Services, Chronicle Features, Creators Syndicate, and the United Features Syndicate.

table of contents

about the authors

David H. Barlow, Ph.D., is currently Distinguished Professor in the Department of Psychology at the State University of New York at Albany and is Co-Director of the Center for Stress and Anxiety Disorders. He is also Director of the Phobia and Anxiety Disorders Clinic and Sexuality Research Program at SUNY-Albany.

Dr. Barlow has published over 200 articles and chapters and nine books, mostly in the areas of anxiety disorders, sexual problems, and clinical research methodology. He has been a consultant to the National Institutes of Health since 1973. Dr. Barlow is past President of the Association for Advancement of Behavior Therapy, past Associate Editor of the *Journal of Consulting and Clinical Psychology*, past Editor of the *Journal of Applied Behavior Analysis*, and *Behavior Therapy*. He is also a Diplomate in Clinical Psychology of the American Board of Professional Psychology and maintains a private practice.

Ronald M. Rapee, Ph.D., is currently senior lecturer in the Department of Psychology, University of Queensland, Australia, and is Co-Director of the Behaviour Research and Therapy Center, University of Queensland. Prior to his current position, he was assistant director of the Phobia and Anxiety Disorders Clinic, SUNY-Albany.

Dr. Rapee has published a large number of articles and book chapters in the area of anxiety disorders and has recently co-edited a book on chronic anxiety with David H. Barlow, Ph.D. In addition, he has presented a number of workshops and conference papers on the nature and treatment of anxiety and stress. Dr. Rapee was recently given an Early Career Award by the Australian Psychological Society and is a member of the editorial board of the *Journal of Anxiety Disorders*. He is a member of the Australian Psychological Society, a registered clinical psychologist in New York State and Queensland, and maintains a private practice.

Mastering Stress

From the outside, Joe looked like a classic success story. At age 45, he owned a profitable business, had a beautiful family, and had just built a new home. Inside, however, Joe felt miserable. Although he stayed at work later and later each night, he never seemed to accomplish enough. When he finally arrived home, his head was pounding, and he yelled at his children so often that they began to shy away from him. Nothing made Joe happy -- not his business, not his family, and most of all, not himself. Each day brought new irritations, until one day Joe looked around and realized that he was hurting everything and everyone that mattered to him.

Stress was ruining Joe's life. He is not alone. Stress is the most common problem facing people in today's complex world. You can't see it, hear it, or smell it, yet stress can threaten both your physical health and psychological well-being.

If you are a chronic worrier, if you push yourself toward perfection each day and then punish yourself for all that you have not accomplished, then you are waging your own battle with stress. Perhaps you are irritable and tense most of the time, and your doctor has said that stress is causing your headaches and upset stomach.

Different people react to stress in different ways. Whatever your own response may be, it is important to know one thing: You **can** learn to master stress and the problems it causes you. Picking up this book was your first move toward that goal. Our step-by-step program will help you identify what is causing your stress, teach you to relax, and show you how to think more realistically. You will emerge calmer and more in control.

The program presented in this book is the result of eight years of research at the Center for Stress and Anxiety Disorders of the State University of New York at Albany. It is the largest research center of its kind in the world. In recent years, researchers at the center have learned more about stress than was ever known before. Hundreds of people who have come to the center for help have followed a program like this one and found themselves much better able to cope with stress. The goal is not to eliminate all stress but rather to reduce your stress to a manageable level. None of us can live without a little stress in our lives.

The Basics Of Stress

Simply put, stress is a state of readiness. It is the mind's and body's way of rising to an occasion and preparing you to do your best. Although the effects of too much stress can be debilitating, stress itself is a completely natural and necessary response, one experienced by all humans and animals.

Stress is not -- repeat, not -- a mental illness. Just as people's heights vary over a wide range from short to tall, people's everyday stress levels vary over a wide range from relaxed to "stressed out." Stress, no matter how extreme, will never make you "go crazy."

The physical and mental responses that constitute stress are useful if they happen occasionally and in moderation. But if they happen all the time, day in and day out, they can have unpleasant effects.

Experiencing a high level of stress for a long time can cause you to lose sleep, feel constantly fatigued, have trouble concentrating, and respond irritably to those around you. Long-term stress can also cause headaches, skin irritations, ulcers, diarrhea, and pains at the base of the jaw (Temporomandibular Joint Syndrome, or TMJ). Stress can interfere with sexual function, inhibiting both desire and ability. Research also shows that long-term stress may increase your chances of later developing heart disease, high blood pressure, diabetes, or immune system problems.

Although this list may look intimidating, you should not add to your stress by worrying about health problems. Being highly stressed does not mean that you **will** get diseases, merely that you may increase your susceptibility over time. Clearly, reducing stress can have important benefits, both mentally and physically.

Are You Ready

The only person who can change your stress level is **you**. Our program can help, but the motivation and the time must come from you. If you work hard, you will be rewarded. People who have completed this program report that they are enjoying life more and that their friends and family enjoy them more.

In the lessons that follow, you will be learning new skills - new ways of thinking, acting, and organizing your life. The key term you will hear over and over is practice. If you practice these skills, and practice hard, we are confident you will learn to master your stress.

To complete this program, you should plan on spending a few minutes each day for about twelve weeks. For the first two weeks you will simply practice keeping records, working to get a handle on the causes of stress in your life and the way you react to them. After that, you will be doing one lesson each week for the next ten weeks. Some people may want to take more time. It is possible that during some weeks you will start feeling better before you have finished the lesson, and you may be tempted to jump ahead to the next one. Try not to give in to this temptation. It is important to complete each lesson if you want to become proficient in using the skills you learn.

It is also important to recognize that life is full of unfortunate happenings - divorce, illness, death of a loved one - all of which can cause stress. Obviously, this program cannot cancel a divorce or bring someone you loved back to life. What it will do is help you deal with your reactions to these situations, so that stress does not control your life. The techniques you will learn in this program can also help you find a more direct solution to other types of problems, such as the small, everyday hassles and burdens we all encounter.

Your First Exercise

It is never easy to find the motivation to accomplish a difficult task, and it is even harder to keep motivated when the rewards are weeks or months away. So before you get started, try these two simple exercises to ease your way into the program:

1. **Think about why you want to change.** What is stress doing to the quality of your life? On the chart below, make a list of all the negative effects you can see stress having. Maybe you lie awake at night worrying about everything you have to do, bicker with your spouse or make careless errors at work. Examine your life honestly, and write down the negatives caused by stress.

2. **Think about how your life will be better once you have mastered stress.** Maybe you will have fewer headaches or less trouble with that nervous stomach. Maybe you will be able to enjoy sitting down and relaxing with friends without worrying about how much you have to do.

    On the bottom half of the list below, list the positives you aim for in the future. Make a copy of your list and place it in a prominent place, perhaps on the refrigerator or near your bed. When the going gets tough, look at it and think of the positive benefits you are working toward.

Negatives Effects In My Life Caused By Stress

1. _____

2. _____

3. _____

4. _____

5. _____

Postive Effects In My Life When I've Mastered My Stress

1. _____

2. _____

3. _____

4. _____

5. _____

Self-Control Techniques

Once you have decided to begin this program, you will need something to keep you going. We recommend self-control techniques. These techniques, that you establish when you are highly motivated, will help you to get through those inevitable times when your motivation is lower.

Some self-control techniques are social, enlisting other people to help you toward your goal. Other techniques are material, involving actual rewards or punishments. You may want to experiment with both kinds to see what works best for you.

Social Techniques

Material Techniques

For example, to commit yourself socially, you could tell your friends and relatives that you are beginning a stress-control program. Ask them to discuss it with you and to encourage you from time to time. Better still, you could make a commitment with your spouse or close friend that you will both follow the program. Then the two of you can set aside time to talk about your progress, and you will each have someone to turn to when you need encouragement.

Material techniques are more concrete. For example, suppose that one day you are feeling so energetic that you decide to take up jogging. Immediately before you lose the feeling, you put $50 into a jar and decide that you are going to jog for one mile, three times a week. Each week that you fulfill that commitment, you can take $10 out of the jar, and spend it on something that you really enjoy.

Each week you do not jog three times, take the $10 and donate it to a charity. In this way, you will have used your original motivation to ensure that later on, if you start feeling lazy, you will have an extra incentive to jog.

You may want to combine social and material techniques, perhaps by having a friend or relative issue the rewards and punishments. For instance, in the above example, you may agree to go jogging with a friend. Give the $50 to them so they pay you if you jog three times a week and keep the money if you do not. That way, you can't cheat.

Self-control techniques may sound a little silly or childish, and in fact, they are no substitute for willpower. Still, for most of us, when we embark on a course of long-term change, it is important to do all we can to ensure that we stay with the program.

Some Cautions To Consider

If you have been troubled by stress for a long time, a doctor may have prescribed a tranquilizer or other drug for you. It is perfectly acceptable to continue taking those drugs while working through the lessons in this program. After completing this program in our clinic, about 30 percent of the people who were taking drugs, such as minor tranquilizers, stop needing them. Others appreciate the comfort of having a pill with them if they need it, though they may not need it as often as they did before they went through the program. If you wish to stop your regularly prescribed medication during or after this program, we recommend that you consult your physician. Drugs for stress are discussed in more detail in the Afterword.

Is This Book For Me

Although this program can help many people deal with a wide array of feelings, it is not appropriate for every situation. If you are being treated for depression, you should consult your physician or mental health professional before starting this program. The program is not appropriate if you experience frequent, uncontrollable panic attacks - attacks in which your heart beats very fast, you experience hot and cold flashes, and you tremble and feel as if you are going to faint. If you do have panic attacks, you could benefit more from another program called: *Mastery of Your Anxiety and Panic*. It is available from:

The Center for Stress and Anxiety Disorders
1535 Western Avenue
Albany, NY 12203

Once you have decided that this program is right for you, you will want to learn more about how it works. The next lesson will explain the system and allow you to practice the record keeping that is essential to completing the program successfully. Then you will be on your way to becoming a **Master of Stress Management**.

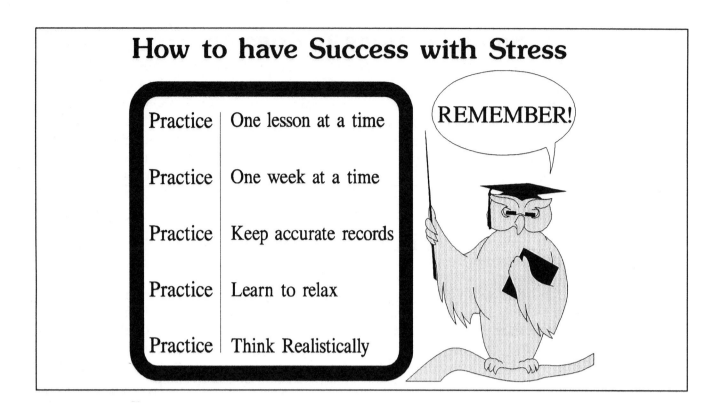

How to have Success with Stress

REMEMBER!

Practice	One lesson at a time
Practice	One week at a time
Practice	Keep accurate records
Practice	Learn to relax
Practice	Think Realistically

At the end of each lesson, we will ask you to complete a short "true-false" self-assessment exercise. These exercises will help you determine if you have mastered the lesson. If you miss a particular question, please review that section of the lesson before you proceed.

Introduction Exercise

Please answer each question by circling either true or false.

1. In order to lower your stress level, you will have to become a completely different person.   *True*   *False*

2. Practicing the skills in this book is one sure way to control your anxiety and stress.   *True*   *False*

3. Motivation is important, but not necessary in the treatment of stress.   *True*   *False*

4. Having other people in your life actively involved in your stress management program is one way to help you practice your skills.   *True*   *False*

5. An excellent form of self-control involves using both the help of others as well as material rewards.   *True*   *False*

Please turn to Appendix B on page 119 for answers to this exercise.

Keeping Records

Each lesson in this program will introduce a new stress management technique, show you how to incorporate the technique into your daily life, and provide you with an assignment to help you practice. Accompanying most of the techniques you will find one or two forms for keeping track of certain events and feelings. Even if you dislike paperwork, do not ignore these forms. Keeping records is very important if you want the program to help you.

The first thing you will need is a folder. As you complete each recording form, put it into the folder. From time to time, look over earlier forms to see how you have progressed. You are sure to be encouraged.

You should use the forms to keep records of each technique for **at least** two or three weeks. It is best, however, to continue your record keeping far longer.

Why Fill Out Forms

Keeping accurate, detailed records is important for four reasons:

1. **Staying motivated.** If you keep honest records, you are more likely to practice each technique as recommended. You will also be able to give yourself credit for what you have accomplished.

2. **Learning skills.** Writing out the details in a structured way helps you to understand how each technique works and how it affects you. You will find this particularly true in the lessons on realistic thinking, where keeping good records is the key to learning the skill.

3. **Identifying triggers.** The things that cause stress are known as "triggers," and they are different for each of us. Some of them are large, life-changing events like those listed at the top of the following page. Others are everyday occurrences, minor hassles that might not bother others but that are legitimately stressful for you.

   When you do not know what is causing your stress, your mind and body's responses can seem frightening and unexplainable. Keeping records will help you to identify your stress triggers, thus giving you a greater sense of control.

4. **Gaining objectivity.** None of us know all there is to know about our own physical and emotional responses. For example, you may think that on any given day, you are either stressed or not, all or nothing. In fact, you probably experience many degrees of stress.

Keeping records will help you to identify the various ways that you react to stressful situations. You may also begin to realize that more of your physical responses are connected to stress than you might have thought. Keeping records of these responses helps make the whole process more understandable.

Triggers That May Cause Stress

Getting married	Buying a house
Death of a close relative or friend	Having a baby
Increased work pressure	Break up of a relationship
Financial difficulties and unpaid bills	Home repairs
School examinations	Car maintenance
Changing jobs	Legal matters

Before you begin to learn stress-management techniques, you will need to learn more about your own reactions. The three forms that follow - the **Daily Stress Record**, **Stressful Events Record**, and the **Progress Chart** - will help in this learning process.

We recommend that you spend *two weeks* recording your responses on these forms *before* you move on to the next lesson. The rest of this lesson will explain the forms in more detail.

Daily Stress Record

The first form, on page 10, is the Daily Stress Record. You may wish to prepare your own version of the form, or take the one we have provided and photocopy it. Then, every evening, sit down with the form and think back over your day. How stressful was it? You will be recording three things in particular.

1. In the **first column**, record your average level of stress during the day.

   The average level means the overall, background level of stress you felt during the day as a whole. Was it a "good day" when you felt fairly relaxed most of the time? Was it a "bad day" when you were constantly tense? Or did the day fall somewhere in between?

   You will notice that we ask you to keep this record using a scale from 0-8, where 0 is no stress and 8 is extreme stress. We will be using this 0-8 scale at many points throughout the program. It is important that you grow familiar with it and practice assigning your responses to some point along the scale.

2. In the **second column**, use the 0-8 scale to note the **highest** level of stress you experienced during the day.

   If nothing significant happened during the day and you did not became more stressed than your average level, the numbers in the first two columns will be the same. It is likely, however, that your stress level increased in response to at least a few things, small or large, that happened. Using the 0-8 scale, write down the number that best corresponds to your highest stress level of the day.

Keeping Records is the KEY to your Success!

Success

Daily Stress Record

(sample)

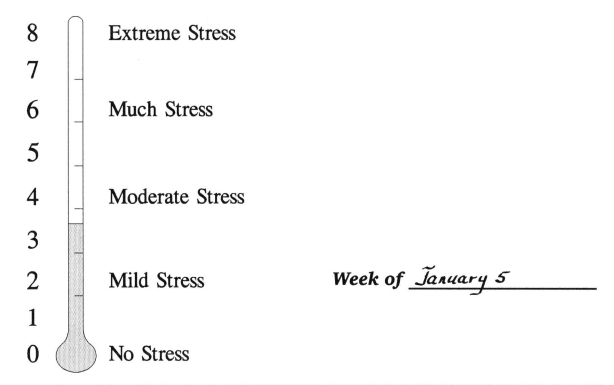

8		Extreme Stress	
7			
6		Much Stress	
5			
4		Moderate Stress	
3			
2		Mild Stress	**Week of** _January 5_
1			
0		No Stress	

Date	Average Stress	Highest Stress	Stressful Events
1-5	2	2	
1-6	4	6	Argument with wife. Late for work.
1-7	3	6	Johnny sick at school.
1-8	4	5	Doctor's report. Lost file at work.
1-9	4	4	
1-10	5	8	Parking ticket.
1-11	3	4	Bought expensive gift.

Daily Stress Record

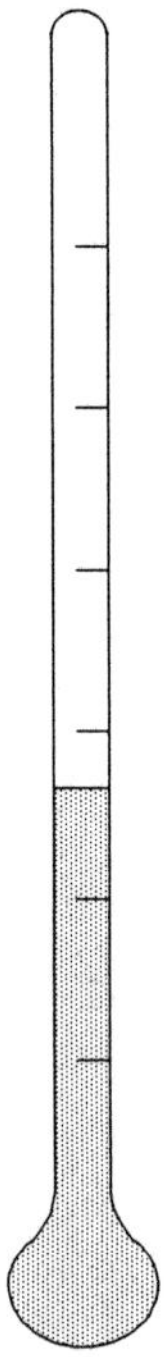

8 — Extreme Stress

7

6 — Much Stress

5

4 — Moderate Stress

3

2 — Mild Stress   *Week of* _____

1

0 — No Stress

Date	Average Stress	Highest Stress	Stressful Events
____	____	____	_____
____	____	____	_____
____	____	____	_____
____	____	____	_____
____	____	____	_____
____	____	____	_____
____	____	____	_____

3. In the **third column**, make a note of any major stressful events that happened during the day. This is the place to list the event or events responsible for the highest level you listed in column two.

   The third column serves an important explanatory purpose. Say, for example, that you recorded your average stress level as two on Monday, but it rose to five on Tuesday. If you experienced a sudden rush of orders at work Tuesday, or returned home to find your cellar flooded, the increase is understandable. Unless you note the reasons on the form, however, you may not remember later what caused your stress.

This points out an important purpose of the Daily Stress Record. It helps you to gauge your feelings more realistically. When it comes to stress, your mind can play tricks on you. For example, how often have you said on Friday, "Boy, this was a terrible week"? Looking back at your stress records, however, you may discover that, in reality, only one day went badly. In this way, record keeping can contribute to your peace of mind. A sample Daily Stress Record is shown on page 9.

Stressful Events Record

While you can leave the Daily Stress Record at home and fill it out at night, you should carry the Stressful Events Record with you, so that you can fill it out whenever you notice yourself feeling stressed. That may sound like a burden, but do not worry. You will need to use this form for only a few weeks. Its purpose is to show you more about how you react to certain events.

Use the Stressful Events Record **every** time your stress level rises. Some days you may record many episodes of stress, while other days you may record none. You will find a blank form on page 13 that you may photocopy. The following instructions will help you complete the Stressful Events Record.

1. In **column (1)**, note the approximate time that your stress began to increase.

2. In **column (2)**, note the approximate time that the level returned to normal.

3. In **column (3)**, use the 0-8 scale to note the highest level of stress you felt during this particular episode.

4. If you know what triggered the stress, note the event or events in **column (4)**. This column is likely to echo the "major stressful events" column on your Daily Stress Record for that day.

5. In **column (5)**, record the major physical symptoms you experienced as a result of this stress - headaches, nausea, pounding heart, or other symptoms.

6. Finally, in **column (6)**, write down the thoughts that went through your head as your stress was increasing. For example, you may have thought, "I won't make it, I can't cope," or "I'm going to look foolish." No matter how silly the thoughts seem after the moment has passed, write them down.

Filling out the Stressful Events Record will help you identify your own particular stress triggers and responses. After a time, you may notice a pattern to your stress, which could point to a specific problem for you to address. A sample Stressful Events Record is shown on the next page.

Stressful Events Record
(sample)

Date	(1) Starting Time	(2) Ending Time	(3) Highest Stress (0-8)	(4) Triggers	(5) Symptoms	(6) Thoughts
1-5	10:00 am	11:00 am	7	Sales meeting.	sweating, headache	My figures are bad.
1-7	5:15 pm	5:35 pm	6	Traffic jam	tension, impatience	I'll never get home.
1-8	12:30 pm	12:32 pm	3	Lost keys	tension	I can't find my keys.
1-9	3:30 pm	4:30 pm	4	Waiting for guest.	sweating, nausea	Are they lost?

12

Stressful Events Record

Date	(1) Starting Time	(2) Ending Time	(3) Highest Stress (0-8)	(4) Triggers	(5) Symptoms	(6) Thoughts

Progress Chart

As you follow this stress management program, you will want to keep track of your progress. Over the weeks, you should notice a gradual drop in your level of stress. Again, however, your mind can play tricks on you. Because you may not remember how you felt **before** the program, you may not recognize your progress. This is where record keeping comes in. On page 18, you will find a Progress Chart. Tear it out or copy it, put it in a prominent place, and fill it out every week. The information you record on the Progress Chart will come from your Daily Stress Record.

Here is what to do at the end of each week:

1. Calculate your average stress level for the week. You can do this by adding up the average level numbers for each day, then dividing by seven. (If you missed a day in keeping your Daily Stress Record, divide by six - but try not to miss a day!)

2. Calculate your average highest stress level. Do this the same way, by adding up the numbers from the "highest stress" column on each Daily Stress Record, then dividing by seven.

3. Record these two averages on the chart. The numbers in the vertical column from 0 to 8 represent the stress scale. The numbers in the horizontal row from 1 to 18 represent weeks.

After the first week, you will have two results to record on the chart above the number 1. Work out your own system for doing this. For example, you might use a circle to represent your average stress level and an "x" for your highest stress level. Whatever symbols you choose, place them in the appropriate place on the scale. A sample Progress Chart is on page 17.

On the sample chart, notice that the **average stress level** taken from the sample Daily Stress Record on page 9 is **3.6** (a total of *25* divided by *7* days) for the first week. The **average highest stress level** from page 9 is **5** (*35* divided by *7* days) for the first week. Points for weeks 2, 3, and 4 are examples of what might happen next.

Lesson Summary

You are now on your way to leading a less stressful life. We cannot emphasize enough the importance of keeping good records. In this lesson we discussed why keeping good records is important to successfully managing stress. We then introduced three records that you will be completing for the next two weeks. The Daily Stress Record should be completed at the end of each day and is a record of your average stress and highest level of stress for each day. The Stressful Events Record is one that you will carry with you during the day and record each event that causes your stress level to increase. This form may look somewhat intimidating, but it is not difficult to master. You will do fine and will learn about those things that are stressful in your life. The last form introduced was the Progress Chart. This is only one form that you will make entries on at the end of each week. Determine a convenient time each week to complete this form. As we work together as a team, we are confident that you will be able to reduce the amount of stress in your life. We are encouraged by others who have been successful in this program. We are also encouraged by your willingness to begin this program and make positive changes in your life. Good luck keeping records for the next two weeks!

Assignment for Lesson 1

For the next two weeks, practice using the Daily Stress Record and the Stressful Events Record every day. At the end of each week, fill out the Progress Chart. After two weeks, you will be familiar with the forms and ready to move on to learning more about stress and about specific stress management techniques. Remember that these two weeks are important to your success in this program. **Do Not** rush on to Lesson 2 before you have completed this two-week assignment.

Keeping Records helps you REMEMBER!

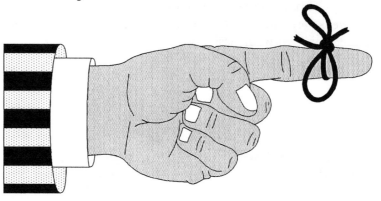

 ## Lesson 1 Exercise

Please answer each question by circling either true or false.

6. Keeping formal records of your behavior in stressful situations should be done for at least two weeks.　　　　*True*　　*False*

7. It is often easy to overlook stress triggers in your life, which can make your stressful feelings increase.　　　　*True*　　*False*

8. Most emotional reactions are all-or-none events that happen with almost equal intensity.　　　　*True*　　*False*

9. The Daily Stress Record is meant to be used to record your major stressful events of each day.　　　　*True*　　*False*

10. Each time you experience an increase in your level of stress, you should note it on the Stressful Events Record.　　　　*True*　　*False*

11. The averages of the background stress level and highest stress level for each week should be graphed on the Progress Chart.

Please turn to Appendix B on page 119 for answers to this exercise.

PROGRESS CHART *(sample)*

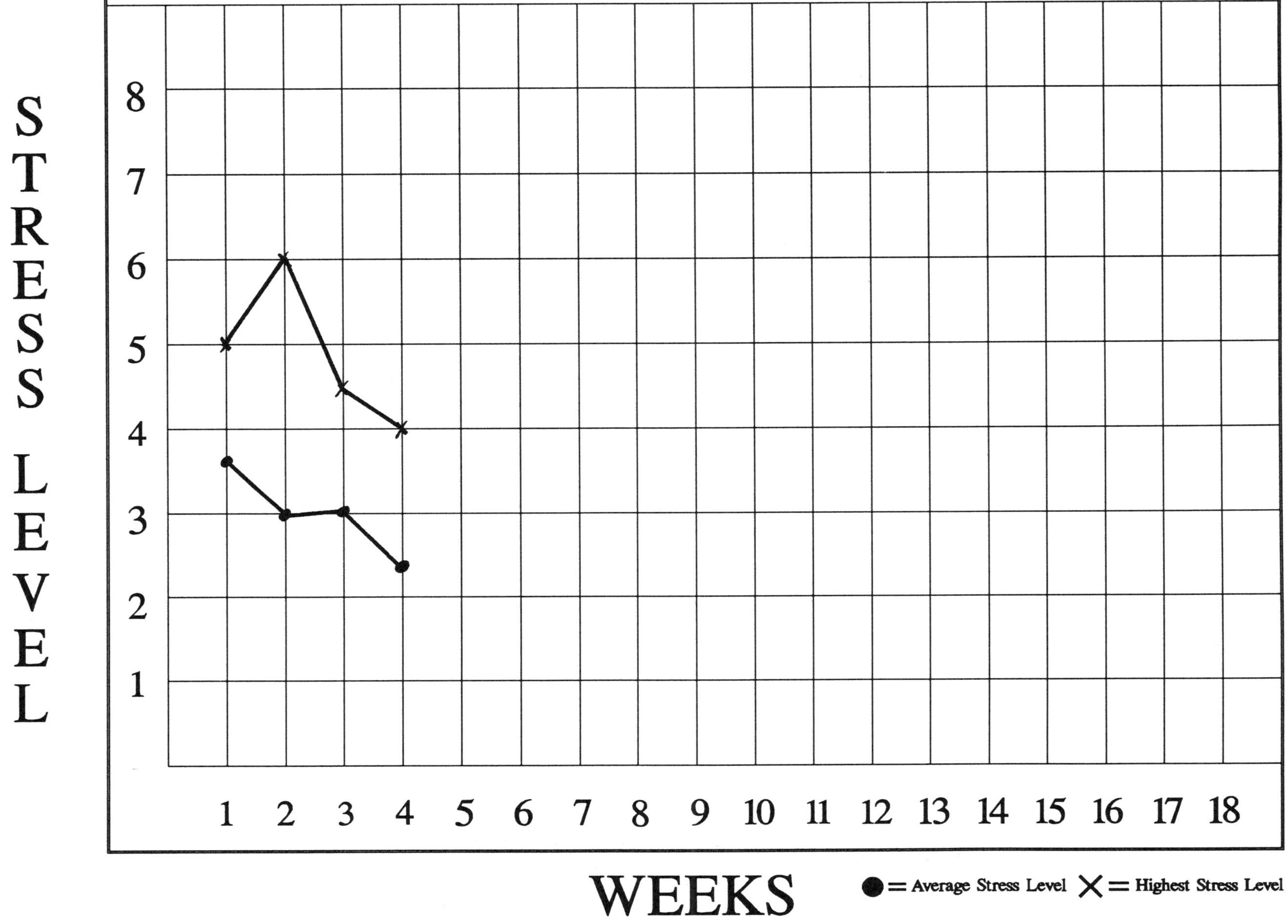

STRESS LEVEL
8
7
6
5
4
3
2
1
1 2 3 4 5 6 7 8 9 10 11 12 13 14 15 16 17 18
WEEKS
● = Average Stress Level
X = Highest Stress Level

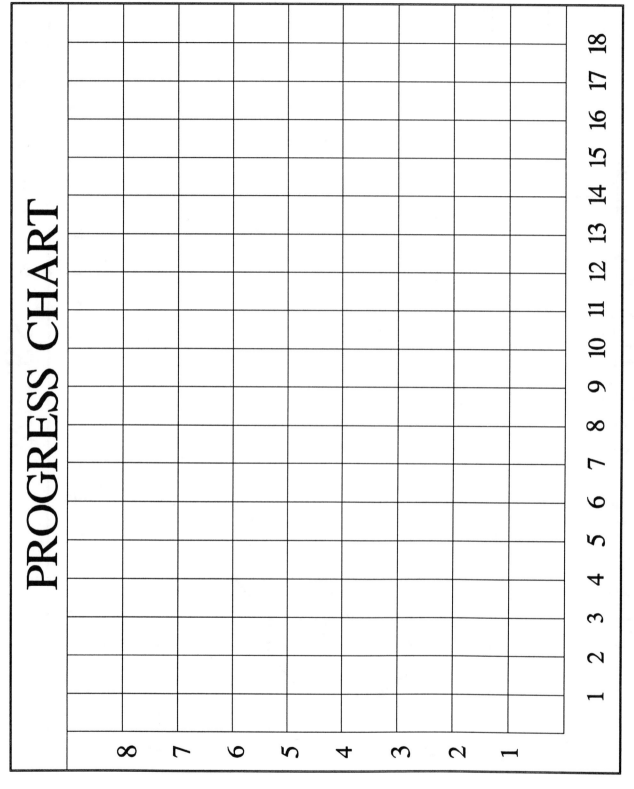

PROGRESS CHART

STRESS LEVEL

8
7
6
5
4
3
2
1

WEEKS

1 2 3 4 5 6 7 8 9 10 11 12 13 14 15 16 17 18

● = Average Stress Level   ✗ = Highest Stress Level

Understanding Stress

Welcome back. Now that you have practiced keeping records of your responses to stress, you are ready to learn more about it. After this, you will be ready to practice some skills for managing stressful situations. As you learned in the introduction, stress is a natural response to a threat or challenge. When you are feeling stressed, your emotions may seem as out of control as a monster in a horror movie. The responses of both your mind and body are, however, logical and predictable. Learning more about them can help you regain your feeling of control.

Stress is a natural occurrence and has a very useful function. Let's say, for example, that you were going to be a contestant on a television quiz show. If you felt no stress at all, you may not prepare for the show, and as a result might do poorly. If on the other hand, you felt extremely stressed, you may be too nervous to study and could become confused and distracted when the cameras started rolling. But if you felt a mild amount of stress, you would prepare well in advance, concentrate better, and react faster when the questions were asked.

Why Am I Stressed

If you are reading this book, you may be wondering why other people do not seem as stressed as you do. You need not worry, your stress is not a disease; it's a personality trait, a way of responding. As with any personality characteristic, your general stress level has two major components: genetics and environment.

Researchers are still trying to pinpoint the genetic component of stress. There is most likely not a specific stress gene. A more likely possibility is that you may have inherited a tendency to be a generally emotional person. That may be one of the reasons you sometimes have difficulty with stress. On the bright side, however, this tendency probably makes you a sensitive and caring individual. The genetic factor only means that you may be predisposed to feeling stressed -- you **can** learn to manage the stress.

Much of your stress probably comes from your environment, from things that you have learned over the course of your life. These lessons vary from person to person, but people who feel a lot of stress tend to have two major beliefs:

***They believe the world is a threatening place
requiring constant watchfulness.***

***They believe they don't have as much control as they would
like over the negatives in their lives.***

If you can identify with these beliefs, just remember that it took you a long time to learn them. You are not going to unlearn them overnight. But with hard work and practice, your outlook **can** change. We will not be looking into your past to try and determine what caused your original tendency toward stress. You will not be expected to regress back to your childhood. Instead, you will be learning practical skills to help you control stress HERE AND NOW.

Facing Challenges

When you perceive a potential threat or challenge, your mind and body prepare you to deal with it. The danger does not have to be real; anything you **perceive** as a threat or challenge triggers your body and mind to get ready. Actual physical threats are not the only trigger. Fear of failure or ridicule is enough to cause stress in many people.

Let's consider an example. Imagine that you are walking home at night and your route takes you down a deserted alley. As soon as you enter the alley, you are on alert. Your mind and body are preparing themselves to take action in the event you are confronted with danger. Though it may not be immediately apparent, the purpose of stress is to protect you. If a mugger suddenly jumped from the shadows in the alley, you would be physically ready to respond quickly.

The challenge of deadlines provides another common example. When you have an important report due in an hour and you haven't finished it yet, you feel stress. When your sister is coming to pick you up in a few minutes and your children are screaming and you haven't had time to take a shower, you feel stress.

In both of these cases, the threat is not the deadline itself. It is the fear that you will fail and that someone important to you, your boss or your sister, will criticize you for letting them down. If you cared nothing about these people, you would not have these stressful feelings. But most of us do care; therefore, most of us would feel stress in similar situations.

Understanding Responses

Stress is one part of a continuum of feelings, a range of ways you may respond when faced with a threat or challenge. This continuum extends from **excitement** to **depression**, with **stress** and **anxiety** in between. The four states are related yet different. The one you experience depends upon your perceived ability to cope with the particular situation you are facing.

In any given instance, you may experience only one of the four responses, or a combination of two that are next to each other (see the Responses to Threats and Challenges figure on the next page). An example might be excitement and stress, or stress and anxiety. You are not likely, however, to go back and forth between two responses that are farthest apart, such as excitement and depression. This section explains the characteristics of each of the four responses to threats and challenges.

- **Excitement**. It may seem strange at first that excitement, which most of us consider a positive response, is related to stress. But being excited is simply another way of responding to a challenge. When you confront a situation for which you feel well prepared, you get geared up for it; you expect your performance to be outstanding. The sensations you feel may be closely related to the sensations of stress, a rapid heartbeat, sudden bursts of energy, or a jumpy stomach.

  Sometimes these feelings of excitement can alternate with feelings of stress, so that you go back and forth between feeling thrilled about how wonderful an upcoming event is going to be and tense that it may not work out as well as you hope. This combination of seemingly contradictory

Responses to Threats and Challenges

Control or Coping

More

Stress   Anxiety

Less

Excitement   Depression

feelings is often present, for example, in athletes. Before a big game, athletes often have feelings of both excitement and stress. Remember, the purpose of these reactions is to prepare you for the challenge.

- **Stress.** Sometimes when you face a difficult challenge, you may feel that you could handle it if only you had the time or the help you needed - but you don't and you feel overwhelmed. Therefore, you may be afraid you will fail or disappoint someone, possibly even yourself. You end up feeling constantly pressured to work harder, do better, and be perfect. You feel tense and irritable; your head hurts and your stomach is tied in knots. This is the feeling of being stressed.

- **Anxiety.** If you perceive that something really dangerous is about to happen and you believe there is little you can do about it, you may become anxious. The danger could be anything from a physical attack to making a fool of yourself in front of someone. You are unable to get the upcoming event out of your mind and you worry about it over and over. The more you think about it, the more anxious you become and inevitably you become afraid of losing control.

Although this program is designed to deal with stress, anxiety and stress are closely related. Most people who are highly stressed occasionally have feelings of anxiety, periods when they feel they are losing control. People who are primarily anxious, on the other hand, often show streaks of perfectionism and irritability, the hallmarks of stress. Thus, the techniques we discuss in this book are just as applicable to the anxious person.

- **Depression.** A person who constantly perceives life as threatening or dangerous, and begins to lose hope about ever controlling these threats, can slip into a state of depression. People who are experiencing depression tend to be lethargic and feel that there is little hope that they will ever be able to change anything. They give up trying to cope, and then they feel worthless - sometimes to the point of considering suicide. If you can identify with these feelings, if you are feeling this hopelessness, you should consult a mental health professional. In recent years, great strides have been made in dealing with depression.

Stress, then, is but one part of a continuum. As we discussed earlier, stress is a natural response to a threat or challenge. Individuals react to stress in different ways. These reactions or responses to stress can be divided into three categories: physical, mental, and behavioral. All three types of responses are aimed at preparing you for action. Understanding these three response systems takes some of the mystery out of stress. And the better you understand it, the more effectively you can deal with it.

The Stress Response Systems

The Physical System

The physical or physiological response system includes all the changes that take place in your body when you are stressed. Some of these changes can seem quite bizarre and frightening when they are unfamiliar. But rest assured that they are all natural, important, and above all, harmless.

When you perceive or anticipate a threat, your brain sends messages to a section of your nerves called the autonomic nervous system. This system has two branches, the sympathetic and parasympathetic nervous system. Simply stated, the sympathetic nervous system releases energy and gets the body primed for action. Later, the parasympathetic nervous system returns the body to a normal state.

The sympathetic nervous system releases two chemicals, adrenalin and noradrenalin, from the adrenal glands on the kidneys. Fueled by these two chemicals, the activity of the sympathetic nervous system can continue for some time.

Activity in the sympathetic nervous system makes your heart beat more rapidly and your blood flow much faster and differently. By tightening your blood vessels, your sympathetic nervous system directs blood away from places where it is not needed, such as skin, fingers, and toes, and moves it toward places where it is needed more, such as your arm and leg muscles. For this reason, when you experience extreme stress, your skin may look pale and your fingers and toes tingle or become numb. This is useful, because if you are attacked and cut, you are less likely to bleed to death. Meanwhile, the blood flow has primed your large muscles for action.

The rapid heart rate and fast breathing you experience when under stress helps to provide more oxygen to your body. Although this is important for fast action, the change can make you feel as if you are choking or smothering, and may cause chest pains. In addition, the reduced blood supply to your head can make you feel dizzy or confused, causing blurred vision or a feeling of unreality.

Overall, stress affects most of the systems in your body. This process takes a lot of energy, which explains why you feel drained at the end of a stressful day. It is important to know, however, that your sympathetic nervous system cannot get "carried away" and leave you in a state of "high stress" indefinitely. Your body has two safeguards to prevent this. First, other chemicals in the body will eventually destroy the

Stress Response Systems

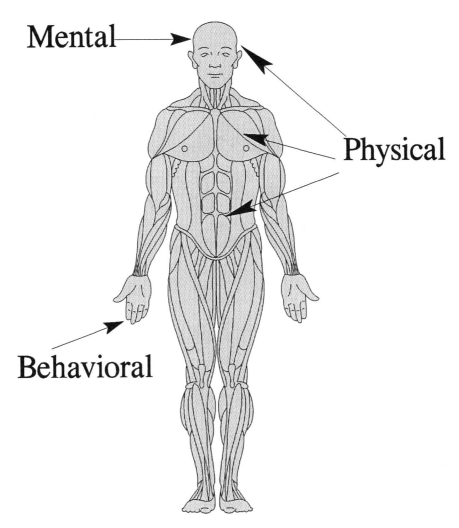

Mental

Physical

Behavioral

adrenalin and noradrenalin released by the sympathetic nervous system. And second, the parasympathetic nervous system is a built-in protector.

When your body has "had enough" of the stress response, the parasympathetic nervous system will kick-in to restore a relaxed feeling. This may not happen as quickly as you would like, but it **will** happen. Your body will not allow your stress to keep increasing until you "explode."

To return to the examples earlier in the lesson, you are likely to feel keyed up and apprehensive even after your office deadline has passed or after you are safely buckled into your sister's car. The reason is because the adrenalin and noradrenalin chemicals take time to dissipate. As long as they are still floating around in your body, you will still feel some degree of stress.

This slow recovery time serves an important purpose in the wild, where danger has a way of returning. It cannot hurt to be prepared. In society, however, we must be careful not to use the lingering effects of stress as an excuse for inappropriate behavior, such as excessive drinking or overeating.

The physical responses that prepare you for action, as well as those involved in calming you down, are largely automatic. You cannot eliminate them altogether, nor would you want to. As we have said before, stress serves an important protective function. It can lead to greater accomplishment and even, under the right circumstances, be enjoyable.

The Mental System

Your body is not alone in preparing for action when you face a challenge or threat. Your mind also gets into the act. The major mental, or cognitive, response is to change your focus of attention. When you are under stress, you tend to scan the environment constantly, looking for signs of threat. On one hand, this shift in attention is useful; if danger exists, you will notice it quickly. On the other hand, you may feel easily distracted, unable to concentrate on any one thing.

As part of this scanning process, your mind considers all the possible outcomes of a threatening situation. In other words, you have a lot of anxious thoughts or, as most of us would put it, you worry. Worrying is one of the main characteristics of people under stress. A little worrying is normal, everyone does it. Many of us worry about the same kinds things. But people who are continually stressed have trouble turning off the worrying. Sometimes they even feel they **need** to worry, fearing the lack of worrying might be irresponsible. Try to avoid falling into this trap! Being responsible is an admirable goal. But if you have reached the point where the thoughts churning through your head are keeping you awake at night, worrying is not helping you, in fact it's hurting you.

Let's apply these components of the mental response to our example of walking through a dark alley. As you walked, you would literally be scanning, looking and listening for possible danger. If there was a sudden noise, even from a harmless stray cat, you would most likely jump. But if a mugger appeared, you would probably spot him quickly. The worrying in this case might take the form of questions running through your mind; "Is he going to hurt me?", "Does he have friends around?", or "Does he have a gun?" To some extent, this worrying is useful; it prepares you for the possibilities.

In the example of the late report, you would probably concentrate hard on the task at hand. In this situation, your focus would not be on scanning, but chances are you would still be worrying; "What if I don't finish on time? What will my boss say? or What would I do if I lost this job?" These worries may be useful if they remind you of how important the task is. But if the worries become so strong that they interfere with your ability to finish the report, you may have started a vicious cycle. Worrying could make you miss the deadline, which would cause you to lose confidence in yourself. Without confidence, you may miss the **next** deadline, and then you would feel even more stressed than you did before. Obviously, you do not want to let worrying go this far.

The Behavioral System

Stress is also likely to influence some of the ways you behave. You may act irritably, or you may start to avoid situations that you fear could be stressful. In fact, to return to our first example, you would probably avoid the alley entirely if you thought it looked dangerous - in which case stress and the anticipation of danger would actually have protected you.

Many people get jittery when they are under stress. You are probably familiar with your own nervous habits: pacing, tapping your feet, biting your nails, smoking, or snacking. Whatever your habit is, you will probably notice yourself doing more of it when you are under stress. Most of these behaviors are simply ways of letting off some of the energy which has built up from your physical and mental preparation for action. Still others (such as escaping from or avoiding unpleasant situations) are there to protect you. The rest may be individually learned ways of trying to calm down.

As with the other response systems, these behaviors are generally harmless and may even be beneficial when realized in moderation. But they can become excessive and begin to interfere with your enjoyment of life.

The physical, mental, and behavioral response systems each have their own purposes. But they also interact closely. Any one system can trigger the whole spiral. For example, you may notice your heart beginning to pound. This, in turn, could trigger thoughts that something is wrong. You begin to pace nervously back and forth. Alternately, you may begin with a worrisome thought about the children which may cause your body to react and then make you want to rush home to check on the kids. Because each system plays a role in the entire stress response, it is important to learn to control each one. This is what our stress management system will help you to do.

Stress Response Spiral

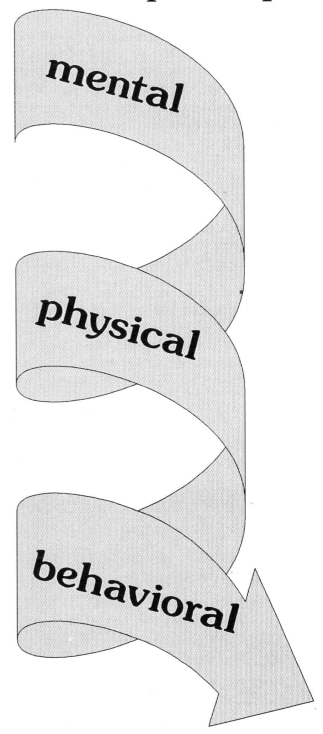

At the physical level, you will learn to recognize tension in your body before it becomes excessive, and you will learn strategies to help you relax. To address the mental component of stress, we will teach you more realistic ways of thinking about situations so that they do not seem as threatening. Finally, at the behavioral level, you will practice new ways of responding to situations. You will learn through experience that threats may not be threats at all, or they may not be as bad as you fear.

Lesson Summary

In this lesson we reviewed the role of stress in our everyday lives. Stress is a very natural, protective response to certain threats and challenges. Individuals react and respond differently to similar situations. Some of this difference may be explained by genetics and some by environmental or learned responses. Stress is but one of four components on a continuum of responses to threats and challenges; **excitement - stress - anxiety - depression**. We have three basic stress response systems; the physical system, the mental system, and the behavioral system. Each of these systems interacts with the other. It is important to recognize each of these response systems and learn how to gain control over each one. We will help you do this in the lessons that follow.

Assignment for Lesson 2

It is essential that you understand and remember the information in this chapter, both now and at times when you are feeling stressed. Thus, your assignment this week is to read this lesson **at least** three times, until you know by heart most of what it contains. Making notes, charts, or diagrams may help.

Continue to monitor your daily and weekly stress levels by completing the Daily Stress Record, the Stressful Events Record, and the Progress Chart. In addition, if you experience any stressful episodes this week, try to think of them in terms of the three response systems. What physical responses do you notice in yourself? Mental responses? Behavior responses? Jot them down on your Stressful Events Record and think about how each one helped or hindered you.

Lesson 2 Exercise

Please answer each question by circling either true or false.

12. The parasympathetic nervous system protects the body by preventing intense emotions, like anxiety, to spiral to extremely high levels. *True   False*

13. It is dangerous for your heart to beat too rapidly or forcefully while you are experiencing stress. *True   False*

14. Even a little stress in your life can be detrimental to your health. *True   False*

15. Stress is a natural reaction or response to possible threatening or challenging situations. It is the only logical response to these situations. *True   False*

16. It is possible to vacillate between a state of stress and anxiety when responding to challenging situations. *True   False*

17. The physical response system to stress may provide symptoms, such as increased heart rate, fast breathing, chest pains, and a choking sensation. *True   False*

Please turn to Appendix B on page 119 for answers to this exercise.

Learning to Relax

Anyone who has experienced stress (and that's everyone) knows that it can take a physical toll. When you are highly stressed, you spend much of your day feeling and acting tense. Eventually this "hyped-up" state becomes so familiar that you do not realize when you start tensing up. Instead, you feel only the end products of that tension: tiredness, headaches, or possibly back pain. Managing your stress means breaking this cycle of tension. To do this, our first mission is to help you **identify** the areas of tension in your body and then provide you with techniques to help you **reduce** the tension.

- **Identification -** Tension, like stress, can be desirable at low levels. For example, you would not be able to write if you could not tense the hand that holds the pen. However, you do not need to tense your whole body, your neck, or your back just to write; your hand is enough. People who have a high level of general stress often tense their entire bodies when they need to tense only one or two muscles. For this reason, it is important to learn to isolate the various muscle groups in your body, so that you will know how each one feels when it is tense.

- **Reduction -** Once you have learned how your various muscles feel when they are tense, you will be able to tell when they are tensing up needlessly. This is when you will want to reduce the unnecessary tension. Reducing unwanted tension (relaxation) is a skill that requires a great deal of practice. It is not some sort of "Psychological Valium," or a handy crutch you can pull out when you are feeling uptight and then hide away until you need it again. Instead, relaxation must be practiced often - at least twice a day at first, for 20 minutes each time. The results will be worth it.

You have probably heard of various relaxation techniques, all with catchy names designed to snare the consumer. Most of them work in much the same way. In fact, you may have already tried some of them. Research has not shown that any particular technique is best for any particular type of person or problem. The deep muscle relaxation technique we recommend here **has** been studied, researched, and clinically tested. It has something more; it has worked well for many people. Give it a chance to work for you. Remember that this is helping you build a valuable new skill. The rest of this lesson will show you how to practice deep muscle relaxation. Although no technique is a magic cure for all your troubles, relaxation is an important part of your stress management program.

Getting Ready

Think of a sport you enjoy - let's use skiing as our example. Remember how clumsy you felt the first time you tried to ski down the beginners' slope? If you had quit then, as you probably wanted to, just think of all the pleasure you would have missed. It's much the same with relaxation. You may not "get it" at first; you may feel as awkward trying to relax as you did trying to stay upright on skis. But gradually, if you keep practicing, you will master the skill and become proficient in its use.

First, choose a time and a place to practice relaxation. If you use a calendar or planner, write it down. Remember to be specific. It is not advisable for you to try and sneak it into spare moments when you are likely to be interrupted. Instead, choose a time when no one else is around or when you can ask others not to bother you for about 20 minutes. Now select a place. Eventually you will be able to do your relaxation anywhere and at anytime. But when you are just starting out, make it easy on yourself. Find a quiet room, pull the shades down, turn down the lights, and sit in a comfortable chair. A bed is okay as long as you don't fall asleep. It is difficult to learn when you are sleeping! We recommend you practice the relaxation skill before your day begins and toward the end of your day. You may need to get up a little earlier, but the few minutes of lost sleep will be well worth the effort.

Deep Muscle Relaxation

Deep muscle relaxation is a process of tensing, then relaxing, individual muscle groups. In this way, you will learn how each group of muscles feels when it is tense and when it is relaxed. You will then learn how to reduce unwanted tension in each one. We will begin with a large number of muscle groups and then, over the weeks, reduce the number, making your relaxation technique shorter and more portable. The chart below lists some of the major muscle groups and suggests ways of tensing them.

Do you have a quiet room and a comfortable chair? Okay, now you are ready to begin. First, spend a minute or two just settling deeper and deeper into the chair. Breathe slowly and evenly, in and out. Each time you breathe out, picture some of your tension leaving your body, like a bird gliding away. Close your eyes and keep breathing, slowly and smoothly. If closing your eyes makes you uncomfortable, you can start by keeping them open, focusing on one spot on the floor or wall.

Suggestions for Tensing Muscles

12 Muscle Groups

Lower Arm	*Make fist, palm down, and pull wrist toward upper arm.*
Upper Arm	*Tense biceps, with arms by side, pull upper arm toward side without touching. (Try to not tense the lower arm while doing this, let the lower arm hang loosely.)*
Lower Leg & Foot	*Point toes upward to knees.*
Thighs	*Push feet hard against floor.*
Abdomen	*Pull in stomach toward back.*
Chest & Breathing	*Take a deep breath and hold it about 10 seconds, then release.*
Shoulders & Lower Neck	*Shrug shoulders, bring shoulders up until they almost touch ears.*
Back of Neck	*Put head back and press against back of chair.*
Lips	*Press lips together, don't clench teeth or jaw.*
Eyes	*Close eyes tightly but don't close too hard (be careful if you have contacts).*
Lower Forehead	*Pull eyebrows down (try to get them to meet).*
Upper Forehead	*Raise eyebrows and wrinkle your forehead.*

When you feel calm and can concentrate, you are ready to start working with your muscles. Keep breathing evenly as you tense and relax each muscle group. Do not hold your breath!

Begin with your hands and lower arms. As you breathe in, make fists and tense your hands and lower arms. Tense them to about three-quarters of their maximum tension - enough so that the muscles feel tight, but not so much that they are painful. Really try to **isolate** the tension to that area. Make a quick mental check of the rest of your body to make sure that other muscles are not tensing too.

Keep breathing smoothly and normally. As you breathe, **concentrate** on the feeling in your hands and arms. Hold the tension for ten to fifteen seconds, about two or three breaths.

The next time you exhale, let the tension go. Relax the muscles quickly. You might want to think of your muscles as **flopping**, the way a rubber band does when you release it. **Concentrate** on the relaxed feeling. Notice how different relaxed muscles feel from tense muscles? Keep breathing normally. After three breaths or so, your muscles should be completely relaxed. You are now ready to start the process again, with the same muscles.

You're kidding! . . . I was struck twice by lightning too!"

After you have practiced tensing and relaxing your hands and lower arms two times, take a break for a minute or so. During this time, keep breathing slowly and evenly. Each time you breathe in, say the word "in" to yourself. Each time you breathe out, say the word "relax" to yourself. Try to picture the words as you say them. If your mind wanders away from the word, gently turn it back.

After a minute or so, move on to another muscle group. For each group listed in the chart on the previous page, repeat the process you used with your hands and lower arms; tensing the muscles for ten or fifteen seconds, then relaxing them for thirty seconds. Keep breathing evenly. Try to tense the muscles as you breathe in, and release them a few breaths later as you exhale. Tense and release each muscle group twice. Each time, focus on **isolating** the tension, **concentrating** on the feeling, and letting the muscles **flop** when you let go. It is important that you take a break after each muscle group, and relax for at least a minute before you start on the next one.

Your entire practice session should take 20 to 25 minutes. When you finish the last muscle group, give yourself some time to slowly reconnect with the world. Relax all your muscles, then gently open your eyes. See how long you can keep the relaxed feeling as you go about the day's activities. Before you end your day, find time to do the exercise again.

Problems with Practice

Everyone knows the saying, "Practice makes perfect." When you are first getting started, "perfect" may not describe your practice sessions. Here we will discuss four common difficulties our clients face as they begin to practice relaxation and suggest ways of dealing with each of them.

1. **Concentrating.** Spending 20 quiet minutes alone is a luxury for most people. They have trouble keeping their minds on the task at hand - namely, learning to relax. If you find your mind wandering, do not despair. You are in good company; this is probably the most common problem people encounter. It is important to overcome it, however, so that when you are truly stressed, you will be able to concentrate and relax.

    Think of your attention as a muscle. Like any muscle in your body, it becomes weak when it is not used much, and it strengthens gradually as you exercise it. When your attention wanders during practice sessions, try not to get angry with yourself. Simply let the extra thoughts that crossed your mind go - release them. You can think about them later; right now, you have more important things to do. Deliberately turn your attention, as you would turn a car, back to the road of relaxation. The more you do this, the stronger your attention "muscle" will become. Once you start enjoying relaxation, your attention will wander less often.

2. **Isolating muscles.** Some people find it difficult to tense one muscle group while keeping the rest of the body relaxed. The only solution to this problem is the obvious one: **Keep Trying!** Like all skills, this one improves with practice. Try not to be too hard on yourself. You cannot **perfectly** isolate each muscle group because the muscles in your body are connected. If you have difficulty, lower your standards. If most of the muscles in your body are more relaxed than they usually are, and the muscle group you are working on is more tense than usual, that is fine.

3. **Feeling stressed.** It sounds like a paradox. Some people feel even **more** stressed when they try to relax. If this is happening to you, it may be because the sensations you feel as your body starts to relax are unfamiliar. You may feel as though you are losing control, and feeling uncomfortable, you stop. This is perfectly understandable. But it is important to realize that relaxing is not dangerous, in fact it is healthy. Fear of losing control is one of the main reasons you may be having trouble with stress, so overcoming the fear is important. You may want to try experiencing the feelings of relaxation in gradual steps. For example, start trying to relax with your eyes open, or while a "safe" person is with you.

    Consider the example of our client John. John was an executive who spent much of his day in a tensed state. As a result, he often experienced backaches, shoulder pains, and headaches. Obviously, deep muscle relaxation would be a big help to him. But five minutes into his first relaxation session, John suddenly jumped up and started pacing. He told his us he had felt as if he were falling, and his heart was thumping in a scary way. He didn't like the feeling, so he ran away from it.

    We worked out a plan with John. He began practicing relaxation by sitting straight up in a chair and keeping his eyes open, staring at a spot on the floor. Gradually he learned to relax this way. He then tried closing his eyes for 30 seconds or so, until he became accustomed to the feeling of relaxing with his eyes closed. Then gradually, over the weeks, he settled deeper into his chair and closed his eyes for longer periods of time. Eventually he could do an entire 20-minute practice with his eyes closed.

4. **Falling asleep.** Some people have the opposite experience from John - they are so relaxed that they fall asleep. If this happens to you, consider it a sign that you may be overtired. Try to get more sleep at night, and try to practice your relaxation at times when you are not as tired, such as the morning. You can also try practicing in a slightly less comfortable setting, sitting in a harder chair or on the floor. Sleep is important, but you are not going to learn much about relaxation if you sleep through your practice sessions.

A Related Note

If you have trouble falling asleep at night, you may find that a part of your relaxation exercise can help. Breathe in and out evenly. Each time you breathe out, let the word "relax" form in your mind. Picture yourself sinking deeper and deeper each time. You may have to do this dozens of times, and you may have to wrestle with your mind to get it to concentrate on the word "relax." But many people find that this exercise helps them fall asleep more easily at night.

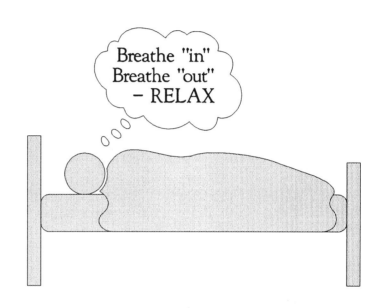

How to Practice

We recommend that you practice your relaxation exercises at least twice a day for the full twenty minutes each time. It is a good idea to keep a record of your practice sessions so that you do not forget or procrastinate and so that you can chart your progress. Try using the form on page 33. On this form you can record the date and time of your practice sessions, and rate how tense you feel before and after you practice. Using the 0-8 scale, which should be familiar by now, rate the tension and how well you are able to concentrate during practice. On the following page, we have provided a sample Relaxation Practice Record.

Gradually, your tension level should drop and your concentration level should rise. If you encounter any problems during a session, or discover any techniques that work especially well, write them down on the chart so you will remember them next time.

In addition to your main practices each day, try to do some "mini practices." When you have a few spare minutes - for example, on your lunch break, in the bathroom, at a traffic light, or during the commercials on television - try tensing and relaxing one or two muscle groups. In particular, work on the muscles that have been giving you the most trouble. Also, as you go through your day, pay attention to which muscles are tensing up, and try to relax them.

Relaxation Practice Record
(sample)

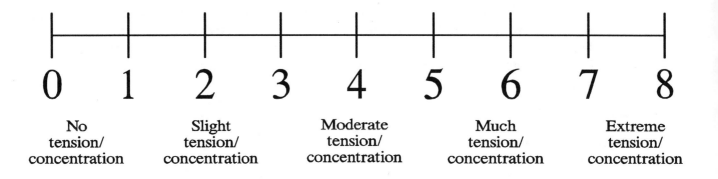

		0	1	2	3	4	5	6	7	8	

No tension/concentration | Slight tension/concentration | Moderate tension/concentration | Much tension/concentration | Extreme tension/concentration

Date	Time	Tension Before (0-8)	Tension After (0-8)	Concentration (0-8)	Comments
1-23	9:00 am	6	4	5	Woke up feeling tense.
1-23	12:00 pm	5	3	4	Having trouble sleeping.
1-24	10:30 am	4	3	5	New attitude toward worry in effect.
1-24	8:30 pm	5	3	5	Feeling good after relaxing.
1-25	5:00 pm	6	5	3	Too stressed to concentrate.
1-26	5:30 pm	6	4	4	I'm so wired it's hard to sit down to start.
1-26	11:00 pm	5	3	4	
1-27	10:30 pm	6	5	4	I feel like I have electrodes attached.
1-28	9:30 am	3	2	5	Woke up feeling more relaxed.
1-28	11:00 pm	4	3	4	

Relaxation Practice Record

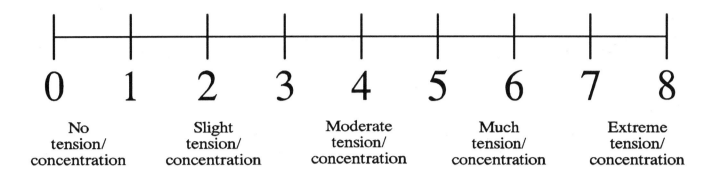

Date	Time	Tension Before (0-8)	Tension After (0-8)	Concentration (0-8)	Comments

Lesson Summary

In this lesson we began to focus on one technique that is significant in controlling and reducing stress - relaxation. Identifying the muscle or muscle groups in your body that become tense is the first step. It is perfectly natural for certain muscles to tense under certain conditions, therefore, it is important to be able to determine what is natural and what is unnecessary. Practicing skills designed to relax particular muscle groups will enable you to relax those unnaturally tense muscles that you have identified. Becoming proficient at this skill is an essential element of this program and your ability to control stress, so practice diligently. Your confidence and proficiency will grow as you continue to practice. Keep a good record of the Relaxation Practice Record of your relaxation sessions. This information will prove valuable later in the program.

Assignment for Lesson 3

Your assignment for this lesson is to practice deep muscle relaxation twice a day, **every** day, for at least two weeks. Of course, if you do not feel you are as competent at relaxing as you would like after two weeks, keep practicing before going on to Lesson 4. Keep a record of your practices. Before each of your first three or four sessions, reread this lesson to make sure you understand all the details. In addition, try to do as many mini-practices as possible. At this point, you can stop recording stressful events, but remember to keep recording your daily stress levels on your Daily Stress Record and keep filling out your Progress Chart.

  # Lesson 3 Exercise

Please answer each question by circling either true or false.

18. Learning relaxation techniques means learning how to reduce tension in all areas of your body at the same time.   *True   False*

19. Deep Muscle Relaxation involves isolating muscle tension, concentrating on the feeling it produces, and then flopping when tension is released.   *True   False*

20. It is important to focus on the word "relax" each time you breathe in during Deep Muscle Relaxation.   *True   False*

21. You should practice Deep Muscle Relaxation at least twice a day for 20 minutes each time.   *True   False*

Please turn to Appendix B on page 119 for answers to this exercise.

Thinking Realistically - Part I

How Likely Is It, Really

Deep muscle relaxation helps you control the physical side of stress. Now we will introduce some techniques for controlling the mental side. If you can learn to control your thoughts, you will have come a long way toward reducing the stress in your life.

You probably think that an event itself determines the way you react to it. That is not true. Actually, your beliefs and thoughts are what determine how you react. This is why two people can react so differently to the same event. Understanding this relationship between thoughts and reactions is critical to learning to control stress. To illustrate, let's look at an example.

Imagine yourself standing outside a movie theater where a friend has agreed to meet you for the six o'clock show. You arrive on time at 5:45, and you stand outside the theater. Try to picture the scene - traffic going by, people walking past laughing and talking, the temperature of the air, and the sounds and smells around you. Imagine yourself pacing slowly up and down, looking at the advertisements, watching the other people going in. It's now 5:50, then 5:55, and still there is no sign of your friend. Finally, the clock strikes six. The last people have gone in, the movie has probably started, and still your friend is not there. Stop and ask yourself how would you **feel**. What would your actual emotion be, and how strong would it be on the 0-8 scale? Most people report that they are either very worried or very angry (maybe around a "6" on the scale).

Now imagine that your friend comes running around the corner and before you can say anything, says, "I'm so sorry I'm late, but there was an accident right in front of me and I had to help the people while they were waiting for the police and paramedics." Now how would you feel? At this point, most people report that their anger or worry disappears.

If we asked you what caused your emotions as you stood outside the theater, you would most likely answer that you were worried or angry because your friend was late. But let's look at what happened. Obviously, your friend was late before she showed up. But she was still late even after she arrived. In other words, the **event** did not change; your friend was late in both cases. However, your **emotion** changed dramatically. So it could not have been the event that directly caused your emotion. What changed was your interpretation of the event, your **thoughts** about it. These thoughts are what caused your emotion.

Before your friend showed up, you might have been thinking such thoughts as, "She's always late," or "She's so irresponsible." Those thoughts would have made you feel angry. If you were thinking, "I hope she's okay," or "Maybe she had an accident," or perhaps "Did I come at the wrong time?", you probably would have felt anxious. After your friend arrived and you realized that she was neither hurt or irresponsible, your thoughts immediately changed. In other words, it was your thoughts about your friend's lateness - not the lateness itself - that caused you to feel worried or anxious. If you could have changed your thoughts while you were waiting, you could have saved yourself a lot of unnecessary stress. That is exactly what you will be learning to do in this lesson and the next.

Changing Your Thoughts

In order to think realistically, you should understand these five points:

1. Your emotional reactions are the **direct** result of your thoughts and beliefs about an event, not the results of the event itself. Two people react differently to the same event because they think differently about it. Let's say that two men go up in a plane for a skydiving lesson. One man happily jumps out of the plane because he thinks he will experience a great feeling of freedom. The other decides to stay inside the plane because he thinks he might get killed. The relationship between events and reactions is shown below:

2. Extreme emotions are caused by extreme beliefs. By changing your extreme beliefs, you can learn to control your emotional reactions.

3. Many of your thoughts and beliefs are automatic, which means that they come very fast and you may not be consciously aware of them. So, it may seem that you just react, without any thought. But the thoughts are really there. It just takes time and practice to identify them.

4. Though it is not easy, it **is** possible to learn to control your thoughts and thus control your emotional reactions. Most people who are troubled by stress believe they have no control over their reactions. But, as you have learned, this simply is not true. Your thoughts and beliefs are not easy to change; you have spent many years developing them and they have become a part of you. But you **can** change them. Once again, the key is **practice**.

5. Realistic thinking is not the same as positive thinking. Positive thinking asks you to look through rose-colored glasses and see the world as a wonderful place. But we all know the world is not always wonderful; this is why positive thinking never lasts long. Realistic thinking, in contrast, asks you to look at situations rationally and objectively.

Overestimating Probability

People who are highly stressed tend to make two errors in thinking. First, they overestimate how likely it is that an unpleasant event will happen (overestimating the probability). Second, they overestimate how bad the consequences will be if that event does happen. In this lesson we will examine the first of these errors. We will discuss the second in the next lesson.

No doubt you can think of times in your own life when you have overestimated the probability of something bad happening. For example, if your boss says he wants to talk with you, you may immediately think, "He's going to yell at me." If your spouse is late coming home, you may immediately think, "She's had an accident." Or if you are asked to take on a new responsibility, you may think, "I won't be able to do it."

In each of these examples, you are assuming a 100 percent probability. By thinking that your boss is definitely (100 percent) going to yell at you, you are thinking that there is no other reason your boss might want to talk with you. Realistically though, there are many reasons your boss may want to talk with you, only one of which involves anger. So you are overestimating.

You may be overestimating even if you are not assuming that an unpleasant event is going to happen (100 percent probability). For example, you may not think that your spouse has definitely had an accident, but you may still think that it is very probable, say 30 percent. But is there really a 30 percent chance that any given car on the road will have an accident? No. The real chance is probably less than 1 percent.

Overestimating probability does not apply only to worrying, it can also apply to emotions such as depression or anger. If your neighbor is playing his stereo loudly, you may think, "He's just doing this to annoy me." Actually, however, the realistic probability that annoying you is your neighbor's motive is much less than 100 percent. If you can learn to estimate probabilities more realistically, you can reduce your stress.

Changing Your Estimates

To change the way you think, you must first learn to **identify** your thoughts. You can do this by asking yourself questions. Each time you notice your stress level increasing, ask yourself, "What's making me feel this way?" Let's say a business meeting has just been scheduled for this afternoon, and you are worried about it. Immediately ask yourself, "Why am I worried?" If you answer, "Because there is a meeting," remind yourself that events do not cause feelings. Ask a more specific question: "What is it about this meeting that is making me worried?" You may answer something like, "I might have to present a report." Now you have managed to identify a belief.

It is very important that you be **totally honest** when you are trying to identify your thoughts and beliefs. Sometimes when you ask yourself a question, the answer may seem so silly that you will not want to admit that you actually had such a thought. But much of our stress is caused by silly beliefs - and they stay with us precisely because we never spell them out and realize how silly they are. So having ridiculous thoughts does not mean that you are crazy. Denying that you have them can hurt worse than acknowledging them.

Of course, not all your thoughts will be easy to identify. If you feel an emotion and cannot determine what is behind it, try to guess a few likely thoughts. The simple process of considering and rejecting these possibilities may lessen your stress, or may lead you to the thought that is really causing your emotion.

Once you have identified your initial thought, the next step is to ask yourself, "How likely do I **really** think it is that this will happen?" The lower the realistic probability, the less intense your emotion usually will be. For example, if your spouse is late and your initial thought is that he or she has had an accident, you will be far more worried if you think there is a 50 percent chance of an accident than if you think there is only a 5 percent chance.

The goal is to find an estimate that is as low as possible. But you must really **believe** it. If you tell yourself that there is no chance your spouse has had an accident, even though you believe deep down that there is a good chance, you will not reduce your level of stress. You need a realistic view of the situation. Two techniques may help you; looking at the evidence and searching for alternatives.

Looking at the Evidence

Everyone knows the difference between real evidence and wild imaginings. But people who are highly stressed tend to ignore the positive evidence and focus only on the negative. If you are aware of this common tendency, you can try to change it.

"Now stay calm . . . Let's hear what they said to Bill."

Say your spouse is late and you are trying to determine the realistic probability that he or she has been involved in an accident. You may ask yourself, "How many cars are on the road in the city tonight?" Perhaps you estimate 10,000 cars. "How many of those are likely to have an accident?" Perhaps two. That means there is a 2 in 10,000 chance that your spouse will have an accident - no doubt much lower than you originally thought.

Then look at other evidence by asking yourself more questions. "How many times in the past has my spouse been home late?" "How many of those times were because of an accident?" "Is my spouse generally a good driver?" "Would I have heard by now if he or she had been in an accident?"

Remember not to focus on the negative. Maybe your spouse did have an accident once and came home late. But what about the 50 times he or she has been late for other reasons? If you focus on the one time and ignore the 50, you are not thinking realistically. Chances are, once you have examined all the evidence, your initial thought will not seem nearly as likely as it did at first.

Consider Alternatives

Another way to learn to think more realistically is to think of all the possibilities, not just the one that initially worries you. For example, why, apart from an accident, might your spouse be late? List the possibilities: he or she got caught in traffic, had a flat tire, met some friends, or maybe he or she had to finish a project. You know your spouse's habits. Does he or she often lose track of time? Does he or she like to work late because the office is quiet after others go home? Clearly, an accident is only one of a large number of possible reasons for your spouse's lateness. There is little use focusing on one negative possibility if so many other events are equally possible.

By examining the realistic evidence and listing all the possibilities, you should be able to convince yourself that, while your spouse may have had an accident, the probability is actually very, very low. If you really come to believe this, your stress will decrease.

Recording Your Thoughts

No one said it would be easy to change your thoughts. It is not enough to read through this lesson and say, "Okay, I'll think more realistically in the future." Your negative thoughts are deeply ingrained in you; they come automatically before you can stop them. If you want to replace them with realistic thoughts, you will have to make a commitment to regular, formal practice. The way to do this is to write down your thoughts and then **challenge** each one. How probable is it? Writing out your thoughts may seem tedious at first, but it is the best way to identify your thoughts and examine them objectively.

On page 41 is the Realistic Thinking Sheet, a form for recording your thoughts and your responses to them. The form is a bit trickier than the others you have used, and it is important that you use it correctly. If you read the instructions below carefully and consider the examples and the case samples that follow, you will soon be an expert at using the form.

1. In the **first column**, record the **event** - the thing that triggered your feelings of stress, tension or anger. Include only the event, not your feelings about it. For example, in this column you would put "job interview tomorrow," not "doing badly at the job interview."

2. In the **second column**, record your **initial** thought or belief. Ask yourself, "What is it about this event that bothers me?" Remember to be totally honest about identifying this belief, even if it sounds silly.

3. In the **third column**, gauge the intensity of your emotions using the 0-8 scale. How worried, angry, or depressed are you as you start thinking about this event?

4. The **fourth column** is the most important. In it, you should record the realistic **probability** that the outcome you are thinking about will occur. Take what you have written in the second column and ask, "Realistically, how likely is it that it will happen." In doing this, examine the evidence and look for alternative possibilities.

5. Now that you have determined the realistic probability, how intense are your emotions about the event? Record that number in **column five**. Ideally, having determined the realistic probability should make the intensity lower than it was in the second column.

When To Do the Exercise

The realistic thinking sheet is designed to be filled out each time you notice yourself reacting emotionally to an event. Make some copies of the sheet and carry it with you. When you feel your stress rising, fill out the form immediately if you can. If you can't, do it as soon as possible - no later than the end of the day. Write down your thoughts and challenge each one.

Your goal is to reach a stage where you automatically interpret events realistically, rather than automatically seeing them in a threatening way. In other words, you will eventually be able to do your realistic thinking while the event is happening. At first, however, most people stumble through a stressful event any way they can, then sit down later to try to think more realistically about it. This will not reduce your stress during the day, but it does give you practice. Next time, you will be able to start your realistic thinking a little sooner.

If, like most of us, you have some continuing worries - money, your children's health, job pressures - practice realistic thinking on those as well. Long-term worries provide a good chance to try changing your thinking **during the event**; in other words, while you are worrying, instead of later.

Case Study

Sharon wanted to reduce her work schedule from five days to four days a week. But when she thought about approaching her boss with this request, she felt very anxious (6 on the 0-8 scale). First, she asked herself, "What is it that worries me?" Her answer (her initial thought) was that her boss might say no. Then she realized that she was assuming there was a very strong chance (perhaps 80 percent) that her boss would say no - and as soon as she recognized that thought, she knew she was overestimating.

To come up with a more realistic estimate, Sharon first looked at the evidence. "I am a good worker, and my boss doesn't want to lose me," she thought. "This place is not so terribly busy; it could live without me one day a week. There's another person to cover when I'm not here. Two other people in the company are working four days a week." Next, she looked at the alternatives, at what her boss might say. "Maybe she'll say no," Sharon thought. "But maybe she'll say yes. Or she'll say she'll think about it. Maybe she'll say we can try it temporarily and see if it works."

By challenging her initial thoughts in this way, Sharon realized that her earlier estimate - that there was an 80 percent chance her boss would say no - was much too high. She decided that the realistic probability was more likely 30 percent. This new way of looking at the situation helped her stress level decrease, from a "6" to a "3". Below is Sharon's Realisitic Thinking Sheet for her work situation as well as other examples from her week.

Realistic Thinking Sheet *(Sharon's Sample)*				
Event	Initial Thought	Emotion (0-8)	Realistic Probability (0-100)	Emotion (0-8)
Want to ask boss for one day off per week	He will say no	6	30	3
Cooking for dinner party	They will hate my cooking	5	2	2
School called about son	He has had an accident	8	10	4
Noise in house at night	It is a burglar	7	1	2

Realistic Thinking Sheet

Event	Initial Thought	Emotion (0-8)	Realistic Probability (0-8)	Emotion (0-8)

Lesson Summary

In this lesson we distinguished between positive thinking and realistic thinking. Positive thinking is short lived. Realistic thinking, on the other hand, is a systematic planned approach to deal with our thoughts and beliefs about certain events that take place. Remember, controlling your reaction to the event is far more important than the event itself. Your emotional reactions are directly related to your thoughts and beliefs about an event, not the results of the event. Evaluating the probability of an unpleasant event and identifying all of the possible outcomes can help you reduce your level of stress. As we have mentioned before, practice is the key. Practice recording your thoughts on the Realistic Thinking Sheet that you carry with you. You will be amazed at the results of doing this after just the first week.

Assignment for Lesson 4

Practice recording your thoughts and estimating realistic probabilities for at least one week before you go on to the next lesson. If you are having trouble with the process, keep practicing longer. Try to record your thoughts and probabilities as soon as you notice your stress level increasing. Then, at the end of the day, think of any instances where you overreacted to an event but did not have a chance to record it. Record your thoughts and challenge them as if they were happening right now.

Remember, you should still be practicing your relaxation twice a day and filling out your Daily Stress Records. If you are having trouble keeping your records, you may want to read through Lesson 1 again. We highly recommend that you go back in the manual anytime you begin to have difficulty with any of the assignments.

 # Lesson 4 Exercise

Please answer each question by circling either true or false.

22. Your emotions are caused and changed by your thoughts and beliefs about an event, not by the event itself. *True   False*

23. Because the majority of your thoughts are automatic, it is impossible to control them. *True   False*

24. The lower the realistic probability of an event, the greater will be the intensity of your emotion. *True   False*

25. Realistically looking at all the evidence means seeing both the positive and negative aspects of a possible event. *True   False*

26. The level of intensity in the last column of the Realistic Thinking Sheet will ideally be less than the level that had first been recorded. *True   False*

Please turn to Appendix B on page 119 for answers to this exercise.

lesson 5

Thinking Realistically - Part II

So What If It Happens

Welcome back. After a week of practicing realistic thinking, you should feel yourself making progress. You may still overestimate the possibility that bad things will happen, but chances are that your estimates are becoming more realistic every day. While you keep working on that skill, it's time to tackle the other misunderstanding in thinking that is common to people under stress: overestimating the consequences of a negative event. You might think of it as making mountains out of molehills.

To highly stressed people, life seems to pack a double whammy. They believe that unpleasant events are likely to happen, and they believe that if those events happen, the consequences will be absolutely horrible. People who "catastrophize" automatically, expect the worst possible outcome. For example, if these individuals are awakened by a noise in their house at night, they may immediately assume that it is a burglar who is going to harm or kill them. If they are called into the boss's office, they immediately think they are going to be fired.

Most people who assume the worst are unaware they are doing it. Since they have never stopped to identify the consequences they are imagining, the consequences stay at a subconscious level, where they cannot be disproved. In other words, the unrealistic consequences are like the unrealistic probabilities we discussed in Lesson 4. They lurk in the darkness of your mind, ready to do harm, until you bring them out and see them for what they are.

What Would Happen If . . .

You can identify the consequences you assume by asking yourself a simple question: "What would happen if the thing I am worried about really took place?" As we said before, realistic thinking is not purely positive thinking. We have to admit the possibility that negative things can happen. The last lesson showed you that the **chance** of these negative things happening is often far less than you might have thought, but still there is a chance. So the next step is to accept that chance and then ask yourself, "If my worst fears came true, what would **really** happen?" In most cases, you will find that the consequences would not be nearly as bad as you first assumed.

Let's return to the example in which your spouse is late getting home and your first thought is that he or she has had an accident. When you think realistically, you may realize that the chance of this is less than 1 percent. But that's still a chance. So, your next step is to ask yourself, "What would really happen if my spouse had an accident?"

At this point you will be doing something that may or may not come naturally, talking to yourself. You do not have to do it aloud - although there is nothing wrong with that if it makes you feel more comfortable. All you have to do is ask yourself questions and then answer them. Although talking to yourself has a bad reputation, it is actually very useful. You should get into the habit of mentally asking and answering questions as you practice realistic thinking.

Why is Steve late?
Has he been hurt?
What would I do if he
is in the hospital?

When you ask yourself what would really happen if your spouse had an accident, you might immediately answer, "He or she would be killed." What does this answer remind you of? Right - it is an overestimation of probability, and you know what to do with those! It is obvious that most accidents are not serious enough that they kill or maim people. It should now be obvious that overestimation of consequences are simply overestimation of probability that **lie below** your original thoughts.

Asking yourself "What would really happen if . . .?" is just another way of identifying your next thought. Many people find that asking these questions opens a sort of Pandora's box, with one thought leading to another and another. It is important to keep going and identify all your thoughts, no matter how frightening or silly they seem, until you reach the bottom of the box.

If you think realistically, you would eventually learn to cope even if your spouse were hurt or killed in an accident. This may sound callous, but it is a realistic fact. Humans can cope with an amazing amount of difficulty. When you reach the answer that is at the bottom of all the questions you are asking yourself, you will usually find that it is not as horrible as you feared.

The following examples from our clinic show the kind of questioning we have been discussing. Our second case about Tim, is a good illustration about how one question can lead to another and another until the bottom line is reached. In these examples, the questions are asked by experts, but you can do the same kind of questioning yourself.

Irene's Case Study

Irene, a woman in her late 20's, took care of three children in her home as a way of making money. One day, Irene's daughter, Sue, bit one of the children during a game. Irene was worried that the child's parents would withdraw him from her care.

Irene	I'm worried that they will take Robert to another sitter.
Professional	Why would they do that?
Irene	Because Sue bit Robert.
Professional	Has Sue ever bitten anyone before?
Irene	No.
Professional	Do you think Robert's parents would understand that the children were playing a game?
Irene	Probably. They're nice people.
Professional	Do you think Robert wants to leave?
Irene	No. He likes coming to my house.
Professional	So then, looking at all the evidence, how likely do you think it **really** is that Robert's parents will change sitters?
Irene	Oh, I guess around 5 percent.
Professional	Okay. Now let's assume that Robert's parents did decide to take him somewhere else. What would happen?
Irene	That would be terrible! We just couldn't afford it!
Professional	What do you mean you **couldn't** afford it? Would you starve?
Irene	Well, no, we wouldn't starve, but it would be hard.
Professional	How much do Robert's parents pay you each week?
Irene	About $50.
Professional	Do you and your family buy little luxuries or do extra things that cost money - like going out to dinner or renting videos or eating ice cream and cookies?
Irene	Sure, we do things like that.
Professional	So if you lost $50 a week from Robert, could you cut back on a few of those things to save money?
Irene	I guess so. It probably wouldn't be that hard.
Professional	So again, if Robert's parents changed sitters, how hard would that be?
Irene	I guess it wouldn't be as bad as I first thought. We could just cut back on a few things until I found someone to take his place. There are a lot of families looking for day care.

Tim's Case Study

Tim is a 42-year-old salesman whose sales did not go well last month.

Tim	I'm worried that I won't be able to get my sales back and they will be bad **again** this month.
Professional	How likely is it that your sales will be bad again?
Tim	Well, I know I'm usually good at my job. In the past I've had times when my sales went down for one month but then went back up the next month. So another bad month isn't very likely - maybe 10 percent.
Professional	Let's assume they **are** down again this next month. What would happen?
Tim	My boss would fire me.
Professional	It sounds like you are assuming there's a 100 percent probability that your boss would fire you. How likely do think that really is?
Tim	Hmmm . . . I'm generally a good salesman. I know of other guys who have had bad months and didn't get fired. One time my sales were down for three months and they kept me on. So I guess it's not at all likely that I would get fired - maybe 1 percent.
Professional	Okay. But let's not stop there. What would happen it you **did** get fired?
Tim	That would be awful.
Professional	Why? What would really happen?
Tim	Well, I would have to look for a job, but I'll bet I could find one.
Professional	And what would happen if you didn't find one?
Tim	Nothing much, I guess. I have some money saved up, so I could live okay for a while, and Icould always get unemployment. And eventually I'd find a job somewhere.
Professional	So, in other words, there seems to be only a small chance that your sales will be down again this month. And even if they are, there's only a small chance that you would get fired. And even if you did, you would probably find another job soon, and even if you didn't, you would survive. So it doesn't sound as bad as it first seemed. How much stress do you feel now?
Tim	Not much at all.

Sally's Case Study

Sally is a 45-year-old real estate agent.

Sally	My mother is always calling just when I'm in the middle of doing something important and it makes me so angry, I find that I get short with her.
Professional	Let's try and look at what you just said in a more realistic way. When you say that she **always** calls in the middle of something, it implies 100% of the time. Is that true? How likely is it really that she will call when you are doing something important?
Sally	Well, I suppose that when I think back over the last 10 times she's called, most of the timesI was just watching TV or reading. There was once when I was making dinner and it burned because she interrupted me. Another time, I was busy with some work I had brought home from the office and she called. I guess that makes it 20% of the time.
Professional	OK, great, now let's go a bit further. So what if she calls at an inconvenient time?
Sally	Well, I know that one of my first thoughts is that she doesn't think anything I do is important. But, before you say anything, I know that is a major overestimation since she obviously doesn't know what I'm doing when she calls. However, I suppose I also think that it's a major interruption and inconvenience to have to stop at that point.
Professional	Go on. What is the chance that it is a **MAJOR** inconvenience?
Sally	When I was doing my work, I forgot what I was up to and it took me 10 minutes to work it out again. I guess that's not so bad - it's only 10 minutes. And when the dinner burned, it was really not too bad, just a little burned. Part of that was my fault anyway, because I could have turned the stove down before I went to the phone.
Professional	So, it sounds like quite a small chance that it would be a major inconvenience, even if your mother does interrupt you.
Sally	True. And I know what you are going to say next. Even if it is a major inconvenience, it's not the end of the world. I have handled plenty of bigger problems than this at work.

(From this point, Sally and her counselor went on to discuss assertiveness training so that Sally would feel more comfortable telling her mother she could not talk now. Assertiveness training is discussed in detail in Lesson 11.)

Putting It All Together

In questioning Irene, Tim, and Sally, the professional was challenging them - challenging the probability that negative events would happen and challenging the likelihood of the dire consequences they imagined. You can learn to do this for yourself. You have already been challenging your probability estimates, using the Realistic Thinking Sheet. We now want to introduce you to a new Realistic Thinking Sheet shown on page 49.

The first five columns of this new form are just like the old one. You will record the objective event, your initial thought about it, the intensity of your emotional reaction (on the 0-8 scale), the realistic probability of your initial thought, and your new emotional intensity. Then, to complete the final column, ask yourself, "What would happen if my initial thought actually did occur?" Write that consequence in the last column. But wait! You're not done yet!

Below the place where you wrote your initial thought, write the consequence again. Now start the whole process over as if **that** were your initial thought. In other words, challenge this consequence just the way you challenged your initial thought. Ask yourself, "What would happen if this new possibility (my previous consequence) really occurred? In answer to this, you will come up with another consequence. Record it, then start a separate line and challenge **that** consequence as an initial thought. Keep going until you reach zero emotion or simply cannot think of any more consequences.

The process will become clearer if you study the sample below that reflects Tim's case discussed earlier in the lesson. As you can see, a single event has the potential to produce a page or more of thoughts. Make several copies of the Realistic Thinking Sheet, and do not be afraid to use as many as you need. Eventually you will not need the sheets at all; you will be able to do all of your challenging in your head. But as with all the other skills you are learning, this one takes practice.

Realistic Thinking Sheet *(Tim's Sample Case)*					
Event	Initial Thought	Emotion (0-8)	Realistic Probability (0-100)	Emotion (0-8)	Consequences
Sales are down for the month.	Sales will continue to stay down.	6	10	4	I will be fired.
Sales continue to stay down.	I will be fired.	7	1	2	It would be hard to survive.
I will be fired.	That would be terrible. I could not survive.	7	0	1	I would look for another job

Realistic Thinking Sheet

Event	Initial Thought	Emotion (0-8)	Realistic Probability (0-100)	Emotion (0-8)	Consequences

Lesson Summary

In this lesson we introduced you to Part II of Realistic Thinking. Here, we have emphasized the importance of continuing your thought process beyond your "initial thought." This is somewhat different from positive thinking because bad things sometimes happen, even to good people like yourself. Honestly challenging your thoughts and assigning probabilities to possible outcomes can help to immediately lower your level of stress. Review the case examples presented in this lesson again to see how this process takes place.

Assignment for Lesson 5

For the next two weeks, use the new Realistic Thinking Sheet to practice challenging your probabilities and your consequences. Keep following your chain of thoughts as far as you can, no matter how silly some of your thoughts seem. Fill out the sheet during or as close to the stressful event as possible. If you truly cannot do it right away, however, do it later. It is still useful to practice challenging your thoughts and emotions. Carry a few sheets with you and get into the habit of turning to them many times during the day if necessary. Soon it will become second nature, and as you fill out the forms you will start to feel more relaxed. Good luck!

Lesson 5 Exercise

Please answer each question by circling either true or false.

27. A person who jumps to conclusions about an event with the worst possible outcome in mind is catastrophizing.   *True*   *False*

28. Realistic thinking is not the same as positive thinking.   *True*   *False*

29. The mind can cope with anything, including tragedies or catastrophes.   *True*   *False*

30. You should not try to be your own professional by examining your underlying thoughts and feelings.   *True*   *False*

Please turn to Appendix B on page 119 for answers to this exercise.

Improving Your Relaxation

By now you have been practicing deep muscle relaxation for two weeks, or maybe longer. Are you starting to find it fairly easy to relax while sitting in a comfortable chair in a quiet room? If you are not comfortable with this yet, do not worry. This is not a contest; you do not have to take the next step right away. Just keep practicing the relaxation technique you learned in Lesson 3 until you can do it easily. You can start this lesson whenever you are ready.

The advanced relaxation techniques that we will discuss in this lesson have four main goals. After listing them, we will show you how to achieve each one.

- **Discrimination.** You will learn to identify more subtle levels of tension in your muscles.

- **Portability.** You will learn to relax through shorter and shorter exercises.

- **Generalization.** You will learn to relax when there are more distractions.

- **Application.** You will learn to apply relaxation to stressful situations in your life.

Discrimination

One of the main reasons for learning relaxation is to enable you to identify tension in your daily life as early as possible - rather than waiting until it turns into full-blown stress. Until now, your relaxation exercises have centered on big, obvious changes in tension. You have been tensing your muscles to three-quarters of maximum and then flopping down to zero. But tension in real life is rarely as obvious as three-quarters of maximum. You can do this by practicing the more subtle aspect of your exercises.

From now on when you practice relaxation, tense each muscle group three times instead of twice. The first time, tense the muscles to three-quarters and flop down to zero, just as you were doing before. The second time, tense to only about one-half of your maximum (moderate tension) before flopping. Finally, the third time, tense the muscles to only one-quarter of the maximum (mild tension) before flopping.

While you are holding your muscles at the one-quarter level and breathing normally, try to think about all the times during the day when you may feel this mild level of tension. The more you practice with these varying levels of tension, the sooner you will start to notice when your muscles tense up as you go about your regular activities. The sooner you notice tension, the sooner you can do something about it.

Portability

Until now, you have been practicing relaxation for 20 minutes at a time (apart from your mini-practices). It is important to start this way so that you can learn to relax deeply. You have no doubt already realized, however, that a 20-minute procedure is not too practical if you need to relax at work or in a traffic jam. To make your relaxation more portable, you can make it shorter. You can do this by tensing and relaxing fewer muscle groups.

We will reduce the number of muscle groups from 12 to 8, then to 4. Although you may choose any muscle groups you like, it makes sense to concentrate on the ones in which you most often experience tension. One of our client's choices are shown below.

Examples of Muscle Groups for Portability Practice
(sample)

Eight Muscle Groups	*Four Muscle Groups*
Upper and Lower Arms	Upper and Lower Arms
Lower Legs	Chest and Breathing
Stomach and Abdomen	Neck and Shoulders
Chest and Breathing	Face
Shoulders	
Back of Neck	
Eyes	
Forehead	

Once you have mastered relaxation with the 12 muscle groups we discussed in Lesson 3, try doing only 8. Perform the cycles of tensing and relaxing in the same way, but repeat them for only about 10 or 15 minutes. Keep practicing with the eight muscle groups until you feel completely comfortable; for most people, this takes about two weeks. Try not to rush yourself. When this technique makes you feel as relaxed as the longer exercise did, try reducing your practice again - this time to four muscle groups. Once you become proficient at this, your relaxation could take as little as five minutes.

When you have truly mastered deep muscle relaxation, you will find you can recognize the slightest tension in your muscles during the day, and you will be able to immediately start reducing it. At this point you are ready to move on to the final stage, **relaxation by recall**. This is different from the practice you have been doing until now. In your practices to this point, you were first tensing your muscles and concentrating on that feeling, and then relaxing your muscles and concentrating on that feeling. In relaxation by recall, you leave out the part where you tense your muscles and simply try to recapture the feeling you had after you let your muscles flop. By now, this should be quite a familiar feeling, both in your muscles and your mind. Remember, if you have difficulty, there is no shame in going back to the longer practices to become more proficient at this skill. It is not always easy to learn new skills quickly, but you can do it.

When you practice relaxation by recall, you should use the few muscle groups which you have been working on up to now. Begin the relaxation practice the same way that you normally do, but instead of tension, simply let your muscles flop. Try to think back to the relaxed feeling from earlier practices and let the muscles you are focusing on feel warm, soft, and relaxed. Between muscle groups, you should still do the mental relaxation as you did before. In other words, each time you breathe in, say the word

"in" to yourself. Each time you breathe out, picture the word "relax" in your mind and try to feel the relaxation washing through your body, as if a gentle ocean wave has swept over you and is now retreating. Breathe slowly and evenly. Let your tension drift away, just as you did in the muscle-relaxation exercise.

It takes practice to achieve a truly relaxed state simply by recall. Once you can do it, however, you will find yourself doing it often. You will still want to practice deep muscle relaxation from time to time, to ensure that you do not forget the feeling. But with relaxation by recall, you can achieve a deep state of relaxation in a few seconds, simply by imagining the word and trying to recall the feeling. You have come a long way from the 20-minute practices!

Generalization

For the last few weeks you have been practicing relaxation, whether short or long, in settings with as few distractions as possible. Over this time, your concentration has been strengthening. Now, when you feel you are ready, you can make your practices a little more difficult, so that you will be able to "generalize" your relaxation to different situations. You will be learning to deal with increased distractions in much the same way that a weightlifter learns to lift heavier weights or a runner to run longer distances. Just like these athletes, you should keep the increases gradual, moving on to harder situations only after you have learned to relax in easier ones. Go at your own pace; no one is keeping score.

Think of ways you can make your relaxation more difficult, and list them in ascending order of difficulty on the blank chart provided below, from the easiest to the hardest. Then try each one until you master it. Here, for example, is one list. Make your own list on the chart provided at the bottom of the page.

Making Relaxation Practice More Difficult (sample)

Practice with your eyes open.

Practice with the lights on.

Practice in a hard chair.

Practice standing up.

Practice with the door and/or window open.

Practice in a busier room of the house.

Practice in a very busy room with the radio or TV on.

Making Relaxation Practice More Difficult

_____

_____

_____

_____

_____

Application

Once you can practice efficiently at home with a variety of distractions, you are ready for the ultimate relaxation challenge: applying your technique directly to stressful situations. Your mini-practices have begun to prepare you for this, just as practice prepares the runner or weightlifter for competition. Like an athlete, however, you should not expect to "win" every time. You cannot beat stress in every situation; some days will always be harder than others. But if you **keep practicing**, you will find those situations that have always bothered you begin to seem less and less stressful each time.

The idea is to think of a task or situation that makes you feel tense. Then, strange as it may seem, we want you to deliberately do that task, or put yourself into the situation, while trying to stay as relaxed as possible. This is the only way to practice relaxation where you need it most - in the circumstances that make you tense. The idea is to go into a situation which makes you tense. Then, **while you are there**, try to concentrate on your muscles as much as you can and recall the relaxed feeling which should be familiar to you by now. Naturally, many situations require your attention, so it is not possible to totally concentrate on your muscles. But by now, that relaxed feeling should be getting so familiar that it should not take all of your attention. As with everything else, practice is essential.

The list below suggests some of the situations in which our clients have tried practicing their relaxation. Take time to think of your own list by asking yourself this question: "What are some of the situations where I am the most tense?" You do not need to choose only those situations which are a particular problem for you. Often it is a good idea to intentionally go into stressful situations and practice relaxing just for the practice. As you did in the last exercise, arrange the list from easiest to hardest. We have provided a blank chart below for you to write down your own list.

Situations That Make Me Tense *(sample)*

Watching a suspenseful movie.

Standing in the longest line at the bank or supermarket.

Doing that frustrating task that you have been putting off at work.

Making that phone call you have been avoiding.

Driving behind the slowest car on the road.

Situations That Make Me Tense

_____

_____

_____

_____

_____

To some extent, the idea of applying your relaxation overlaps with another technique, exposure to stressful situations, which you will learn about in Lesson 8. For now, however, simply make a list of situations and get started. It is a good idea to put yourself in each situation a number of times, so that you give your relaxation a full chance to work. Although no two situations are quite the same, you should find that you are better able to control your stress each time.

Questions And Answers On Practice

Once you have made the commitment to practice relaxation, you will be tempted now and then to loaf. Try hard not to give in to this temptation. Only with time and practice will the skills you are learning really begin to help you. Here are some of the questions that our clients frequently ask about practicing relaxation.

Q. How long will it take before I'm ready to try relaxation by recall in stressful situations?

A. Most people find that they reach this stage about six to eight weeks after they start practicing deep muscle relaxation. It may take longer for you, and that is perfectly fine. Only you know when you are comfortable with each step and ready to move on to the next.

Q. Once I can do relaxation by recall, should I stop practicing deep muscle relaxation?

A. No. Continue practicing, to keep your attention "in shape" and ensure that your skills do not get rusty. You may not need to practice twice a day. Two or three times a week, for 10 to 15 minutes each time should do the trick. If you encounter an especially stressful period, you may find that returning to your original plan (two 20-minute practices per day) helps to relax you at these times.

Q. How long should I keep practicing?

A. All your life. Remember this is a skill and like any other skills you have mastered, you must continue to practice if you want to remain proficient. Practicing two or three times a week is not difficult. Fit the practices into your schedule until they become part of your routine.

Lesson Summary

You have come a long way in learning how to use the skills necessary to control your stress level. In this lesson we have shown you how to focus your relaxation techniques to specific areas of the body throughout the day and during stressful situations. We have now made these "learned skills" portable, so that you can carry them with you. We introduced the concept of relaxation by recall where you no longer tense muscles but try to recall the feeling you remember from practice when your muscles flop. We have provided you with some ideas on how to "generalize" your relaxation techniques to different situations. Think of yourself as an athlete, let's say a stress-player. The more you practice the better you will be.

Assignment for Lesson 6

The key assignment is **practice**. Once you feel comfortable with the basic 12 muscle group practice, start trying one-half and one-quarter tension exercises with the same muscles. When you have mastered that, move on to eight muscle groups, then to four muscle groups, and finally to relaxation by recall. Next, make two lists: one of distractions you can add to practice sessions (generalization), the other of stressful situations in which you can try relaxation by recall (application). Then start working on those techniques.

Remember to keep filling out your **Relaxation Practice Forms,** your **Daily Stress Forms,** and your **Progress Chart.** Also, you should still be practicing your realistic thinking skills.

  # Lesson 6 Exercise

Please answer each question by circling either true or false.

31. The first of the three times you do discrimination training, you tense and relax to one-half of maximum before flopping.   *True   False*

32. Portability means being able to relax in shorter amounts of time by reducing the number of muscle groups tensed and relaxed.   *True   False*

33. While doing relaxation by recall, you tense and relax muscle groups while imagining the word "relax" every time you exhale.   *True   False*

34. It is best to generalize your relaxation skills gradually as you strengthen your concentration.   *True   False*

35. It is wrong to expect that you will be able to relax during stressful events all the time   *True   False*

36. After you get the hang of relaxation by recall and can do it in any situation, you don't need to practice it anymore.   *True   False*

Please turn to Appendix B on page 119 for answers to this exercise.

Thinking Realistically - Part III

Prediction Testing And Other Techniques

Pause for a moment and think about what you have been doing the last few weeks. Can you see the progress you have made in challenging your unrealistic thoughts? Do you feel as if you have taken at least a small step toward controlling your emotions? Progress in mastering stress is more subtle than progress in other areas of self-improvement, such as losing weight. If you have lost weight, friends are likely to stop you on the street and exclaim, "Oh, you look so much thinner!" They are far less likely to stop and say, "Oh, you seem so much calmer!" Eventually the change will be obvious to those closest to you.

For now, though, you should be careful to give yourself credit. Take time out now and then to read over your recording forms, think about recent events, and pat yourself on the back for your progress. If you feel you are progressing too slowly, you may be expecting too much. Even so, it is a good idea to go back to basics by re-reading Lessons 4 and 5, and practicing. This is good advice even if you seem to be going great guns. It may help to brush up on the details. Once you have mastered the basics of realistic thinking, you may want to try some other techniques. We will describe them in this lesson.

Reversing Positions

By now you know that people who are stressed have difficulty seeing events in a clear, unbiased way. Learning to think realistically, then, means learning to see things objectively. One way to move toward this goal is to try looking at your situation from someone else's point of view. Think about the people you know. Is there a person whose calm, logical manner you have always admired? Someone who never seems to lose his or her cool, no matter what happens? You have a choice. You can let people like that drive you crazy or you can get pointers from them. Choose the calmest person you know and try to find out how his or her mind works. Because everyone likes compliments, you may want to start by saying something like, "You know, I've always admired the way you stay calm in upsetting situations. How do you do it?" Chances are, the person will be glad to talk. Or perhaps you already know the person well enough to know the attitudes that keep him or her on an even keel.

Let's say that the calmest person you know is Lee. After you have talked to Lee, experiment with seeing the world from Lee's perspective. The next time a stressful event happens, ask yourself, "What would Lee think about this?" Or try imagining that the event has happened to Lee instead of you. What would you think about that event if you knew that it had happened to Lee? If Lee came to you asking for advice, what would you say? It's possible that you would give very good, useful advice to other people but have trouble knowing what to do when you are in a similar situation yourself. Putting yourself in someone else's shoes can work especially well in three areas that worry people under stress: social concerns, perfectionism, and anger.

Social Concerns

"Social concerns," is a name for something that everyone does; worrying about what other people think of you. For some people, this kind of worry can become so intense that they become afraid to do anything. If you tend to worry too much about other people's opinions of you, try pretending to be those other people. Let's say, for example, that you bump into a co-worker in the supermarket and introduce your spouse -- but you call your co-worker by the wrong name. Immediately, you feel embarrassed. Because you have practiced realistic thinking, you know that your embarrassment comes from a thought, probably something like, "That person must think I'm totally stupid." Now turn the situation around and imagine that your co-worker had introduced you by the wrong name. Would you have thought he or she was completely stupid? Probably not. And even if you had felt bad about it for a minute, you probably would have laughed about it the next time you saw your co-worker, right? So by reversing positions, you have come up with easy evidence to help lower the probability of the statement, "That person must think I'm stupid."

Perfectionism

The desire to do things perfectly causes as much stress in many people as worrying about what others think. Logically, we all know that no one is perfect. Unconsciously though, we often believe that we should be. Again, putting yourself in someone else's shoes is a good way to gather evidence against such thoughts.

For example, if your boss asks you to do a special project, you may immediately begin to worry that your performance will not be good enough. The worry probably results from an unconscious thought such as, "It will be a disaster if I make even one mistake." But what if one of your friends at work did the same project and made a few small errors? Would that really be terrible? Would you think that your friend was a hopeless case and should be fired? Of course not. You would probably think, "It's too bad about those mistakes, but everyone makes them, and overall that person did a terrific job." Once again, reversing positions has shown you that the probability of your original thought - that any mistake would be disastrous - was really very low.

Anger

Many people under stress have a tendency to become angry and irritable for often totally irrational reasons. In many cases, they may hold unconscious beliefs that others are stupid or nasty, and that they themselves are battling everyone else's incompetence. In such cases, putting yourself in another person's position is a very good way of gaining perspective and being able to understand and forgive minor mistakes in others. For example, let's assume you are driving to a meeting and you are a little late. Suddenly, in front of you, a car changes lanes and then proceeds to drive quite slowly. Your immediate response may be to get very angry and to start sounding your horn. These responses are probably being produced by thoughts along the lines of: "That jerk!"; "He's totally inconsiderate!"; "He's purposefully trying to make me late!" etc. Now try to put yourself in the front car's position. Have you ever driven anywhere slowly, perhaps because you were looking for something or your mind was preoccupied? Do you always carefully watch all of the other cars when you are in a hurry? By gaining this perspective, you may then be in a better position to do your other realistic thinking and realize, that by driving behind this car, you are only going to arrive at your meeting a few seconds later that you would have anyway."

Conquering The Magic of Worry

What? There's magic in worry? Not really, but plenty of people seem to think there is. When you worry, all the possible outcomes to a situation swirl around and around in your mind. Often the thoughts keep swirling even when you know there is nothing you can do to change the situation you are worrying about. It's almost as if you believe that worrying will magically change the outcome. That is the so called "magic of worry."

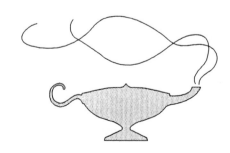

This belief probably comes from the human need for control. Most of us have trouble accepting the idea that there are some things in life that we just cannot control. Rather than accepting this reality, we keep worrying, unconsciously hoping that somehow the worry will change things. This belief may not be conscious, but the worry is. Breaking the worry cycle is simply a matter of convincing yourself that you cannot control everything. Some events are going to happen whether you want them to or not, whether you worry about them or not. Your worrying will have absolutely no effect on these events. But it does have an effect on you; it can make your life very unpleasant.

Think about the last time you took a test or had a job interview. After the test or interview was over, did you lie awake at night worrying about how well you had done? The next time something like this comes up, try talking to yourself. Ask yourself, "What am I worrying about? It's over; there's nothing I can do about it now. I can't change anything, so I might as well get some sleep." This is easier said than done, of course, but it really does help. Once you have convinced yourself that there is nothing you can do to change things, try your relaxation techniques. The combination can go a long way toward calming you down.

A less obvious example involves worrying about your children when they go out in a car with friends. You have already learned that the probability of their having an accident is much less than you might have originally thought. If they are going to drive safely - or even if they are going to have an accident - they will do it whether you worry about them or not. In other words, you worrying at home will have absolutely no effect on their behavior on the road. So you might as well get on with your life.

It may sound simplistic just to tell yourself, "Don't worry." But worrying is like any other habit; the first step toward breaking it is becoming more aware of it. Once you realize that you are worrying because you unconsciously believe that worry will change things, there is only one sensible course: convince yourself that there is no magic in worry. Some things are simply beyond your control - and really, wouldn't life be pretty boring if you could control every part of it? It should not be too hard to convince yourself that worrying changes nothing, except possibly your own peace of mind. If you need reinforcement, try putting up signs. For example, you may want to make a copy of the sign on page 65 that says "WORRYING DOES NOT HELP!" and tape it to your refrigerator to remind you.

If you find that chronic and continued worrying about minor matters is your major problem rather than simply another symptom of stress, you may have a different disorder called "generalized anxiety disorder." If this is the case, you may wish to consult a mental health professional or write for the manual *Master of Your Anxiety and Worry* from the

Center for Stress and Anxiety Disorders
1535 Western Avenue
Albany, NY 12203

Prediction Testing

By now it should be almost second nature for you to ask yourself, "How likely is it?" when you notice a stressful thought. To come up with a realistic probability, you need to take into account as much realistic evidence as possible. But, people who are stressed often have trouble assessing evidence; they focus on the negative and ignore the positive. To help you look at the evidence more realistically, you can try a technique called prediction testing.

In prediction testing, you predict what you think will happen in a certain situation. Then, when it's over, you try to find out whether your prediction came true. By doing this over and over, you build up a store of realistic evidence.

Let's look at an example. If you are going to present a report in a meeting at work, you might feel nervous. As before, your first step would be to challenge all your thoughts. Once you have identified three

Alternatives to Worrying

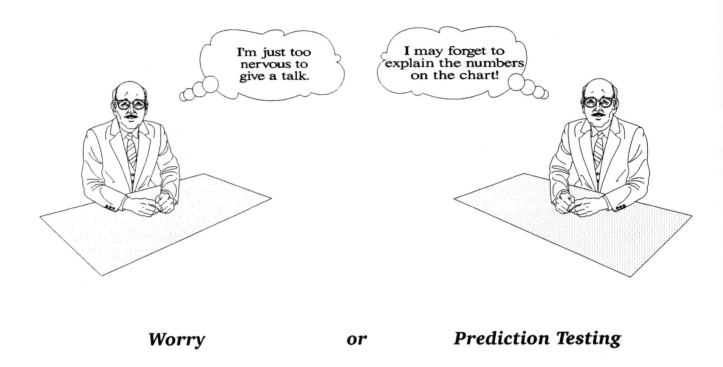

Worry   ***or***   ***Prediction Testing***

or four thoughts that you are having about the meeting, look at them in a new way. Start thinking of these thoughts as guesses, as predictions of what you expect to happen at the meeting. For example, two of your predictions might be, "I will forget my material," and "I will sound as if I don't know what I'm saying."

Now comes the prediction testing. After you have given your report, think about what happened. Did you, in fact, forget anything? Did you sound convincing? You can answer the first question by looking at your notes. Since it may be harder to answer the second question objectively, ask someone you trust who attended the meeting. Try not to pick someone who is such a good friend that he or she will give you lavish compliments no matter what. By asking and answering these questions, you are gathering realistic evidence. It is possible that some of the evidence might be negative. Perhaps a co-worker told you that you could have sounded more sure of yourself. This answer might make you feel bad for a moment, but use it to your advantage. Find out what evidence the answer is based on. Did you say "ummmmm" too many times? Did you stare at your notes instead of making eye contact? Such things are easy to fix once you know about them. Meanwhile, challenge your thoughts about this evidence. "What will really happen just because I didn't sound completely convincing?" Not much, right? Chances are that those who attended the meeting will forget your demeanor and remember your subject. But if you find yourself making negative predictions about this ("Since I didn't sound convincing, my boss won't approve my proposals") you can test them out as well. If your proposals are approved, you have overestimated the significance of not sounding completely sure of yourself. If not, you can ask your boss for feedback on why the proposals were not approved. The reasons may have nothing to do with your presentation.

Chances are that most of the evidence you collect from prediction testing will be positive. You spoke clearly, not too fast and not too slow. You got the statistics right. Everyone liked your chart. And your prediction that you would forget your material did not come true. Look at this evidence and remember it. Next time you have to give a report, you should feel more comfortable.

When you are doing prediction testing, it is not always so easy to test your guesses. For example, if there is no one at the meeting whom you know well, how can you find out how you came across? You have to be creative. If you are worried about your presentation of one particular point, for example, you could seek out someone whose department would be concerned with that issue. "You know that proposal I made for increasing sales?" you might ask. "Do you think it could work?" The way the person discusses the proposal will help you see whether you presented it clearly. If you are worried about seeming credible, you could videotape the presentation (if you need to, you could always make up an excuse such as wanting to show it to a client). Then you could show the recording to your spouse or a friend in a similar field and ask for honest feedback. Of course, there will be times when it is just not possible to get objective evidence for prediction testing. Then you will have to use your own judgment on how the situation went, or possibly not do prediction testing for that event. As you make your predictions, try to be as specific as possible. The more specific a prediction, the easier it is to test. For example, it is a lot easier to test, "I will forget to explain the numbers on the chart," than it is to check a broad statement like, "I will forget my material."

Evaluating Negative Events

At times in your life, things will happen that really are negative. Your boss may ask you to redo a report because it was not good enough. Or your child may fall off a swing and break his or her arm. As we mentioned in Lesson 4, this is the main difference between realistic thinking and so-called positive thinking. In realistic thinking, we accept the possibility that negative things do happen in life. The idea is to know how likely they really are. When a negative event occurs, you will probably have two responses. First, you will probably become quite upset about the event; second, while you may have worried before about such an event occurring, now you may worry more than ever about it happening again.

To help control the first of these responses, your reaction to the event, you need to look at the real consequences of the event. Let's say that your boss told you that your last report was not good enough and asked you to do it again. Therefore, you have a 100% probability that you will write a bad report. Now you have to ask yourself, "What if I do write a bad report?" You might answer, "My boss will think I'm a bad worker." At this point, you can begin to look at the evidence. What sorts of comments have you had from your boss before? Are there other workers who have written unsatisfactory reports? How long have you been working for the company, without problems? From here, you can go on to the standard thought challenges which you are familiar with by now. By doing this, you will often find that negative events are not nearly as bad as they may seem at first. Your second response to the negative event, worrying about it happening again more than ever, is something that psychologists call a "recency effect."

In other words, people remember things that happened to them recently better than they remember things that happened earlier. However, when you do your realistic thinking, you need to take into account **all** of the evidence. You may have written an unsatisfactory report last time, but you also may have written satisfactory reports the previous 19 times. So in this case, the chance that you will write a bad report is one in 20, or 5 percent.

Lesson Summary

In summary, then, prediction testing involves making specific guesses about what you expect to happen in a particular situation. These predictions can be taken from your thought challenges (Lessons 4 & 5), which you should still be doing. After you go through the situation you were worried about, check out what actually happened. And, especially when dealing with negative events, consider all the evidence, positive and negative, taking into account what has happened in similar situations in the past. Sometimes

Prediction Testing Form *(sample)*

Event	Guess	Test	Outcome
Going to New York City	I will be mugged	Go and see	Not mugged, good time
Running late for appointment	I will be late They will be angry I will lose sale	Look at watch Look at faces See if lose sale	Was late Not very angry Still made sale

you can do the checking while you are in the middle of the situation. For example, many people feel nervous when they have to walk into a room where everyone else is already seated. They often have thoughts like "Everyone will look at me." A good test for this prediction is to notice what happens when you do have to walk in late. How many people are actually looking at you? In most cases, it is very few.

Other creative ways of testing your guesses could include asking people questions, taking photographs, looking up records - for example, checking on the percentage of all planes that crash in a year - and making video or audio tapes. Record-keeping enhances prediction testing, as it does with the other techniques you have tried. Keeping records makes the test more systematic and makes you more aware of the results.

Below is a sample prediction testing form. In the first column, record the event that is upcoming (such as, "presenting report at meeting"). In the second column, record your guess or worry about this event. Remember to be as specific as possible. ("I will forget at least a quarter of my material and I will sound as if I don't know what I'm talking about.") In the third column, record how you will test your guess after the event is over. ("Check notes to see whether I forgot anything. Ask Bill how I sounded.") Finally, record the outcome of your test. ("Left out only a small part. Bill said I sounded fine.") On page 63 is a blank Prediction Testing Form for you to copy and use.

Prediction Testing Form

Event	Guess	Test	Outcome

Assignment for Lesson 7

1. Think about someone you know who does not seem to become very stressed. Ask this person how he or she would think in certain situations, using as examples the types of situations that are difficult for you. Next time you encounter one of these situations, ask yourself what the other person would have thought and done. When you become embarrassed or nervous in a social situation, try imagining the situation in reverse. Ask yourself what you would have done if the other person had acted as you did. Practice gaining objectivity by looking at things from another person's point of view.

2. Make a sign (or copy the sign on the next page) to remind yourself that worrying doesn't change anything. Hang it in a prominent place at home or work. Try to identify times when you are worrying needlessly or superstitiously, and tell yourself that worrying won't help.

3. Pick three or four upcoming events that you think might make you feel stressed or angry. Challenge your thoughts and then try to make three or four specific predictions for each event. Work out how you are going to test each prediction. Record the details on a monitoring form and remember to do the test when the event comes up. Use that evidence to help you think realistically when you find yourself worrying about similar events in the future.

Lesson 7 Exercise

Please answer each question by circling either true or false.

37. One effective way to help you be more objective about the events in your life is to view a particular situation from someone else's vantage point. *True   False*

38. Worrying about an event helps to lessen possible negative consequences of the event and is beneficial. *True   False*

39. To properly do prediction testing, you must make highly specific guesses about the outcome of an event. *True   False*

40. Creativity is a valuable tool when devising tests to check your predictions. *True   False*

Please turn to Appendix B on page 119 for answers to this quiz.

Worrying Does Not Help?

"It's the mailman, doc. He scares me."

lesson 8

Reality Testing

Using prediction testing, you have been checking the evidence about a situation after it has happened. The technique works on the **mental** component of stress by helping you to evaluate evidence more realistically. In this lesson, you will learn a related technique that will help you work on the **behavioral** component of stress. The technique is called reality testing. In reality testing, you intentionally put yourself into situations that make you nervous or stressed in order to find out if what you were expecting really happens. But try not to get stressed about the idea of reality testing! You will not have to plunge right into the situations that bother you most. We will help you through the testing in gradual steps.

Everyone knows that the best way to learn something is to experience it firsthand. How many parents complain that their children have to learn from their own mistakes? Yet most of us tend to avoid the types of situations that have caused us stress in the past and therefore, we never learn to deal with them. Or, to look at it another way, your thoughts and beliefs about some situations are so automatic and ingrained that no amount of challenging or talking to yourself will help. In these cases, the only way to overcome your stress is to face the situation you have been avoiding. Deliberately expose yourself to it.

Here is an example to help you understand reality testing. Imagine a new teacher facing the first day of school. Let's say this teacher is a young woman who has just graduated from college. The night before classes start, she lies awake worrying. When she finally falls asleep, she dreams about all the things that might go wrong. She arrives at school the next morning feeling very stressed As the time of the students' arrival grows closer and closer, her stress level gets higher and higher. She feels extremely nervous as she stands outside the door of her new classroom. When she walks inside to begin teaching, her stress rockets to its highest level yet. The teacher wants to run away and hide, but she stays and begins the lesson.

After an hour has gone by, she realizes that she is feeling fairly comfortable. Still, at home that night she gets nervous when she thinks about teaching again. The next day as she opens the classroom door, she feels some stress -- but it does not rise as high, or last as long, as it did the day before. Her experience has shown her that once she starts teaching, she will be fine. As the days and weeks pass and the teacher keeps going into the classroom every day, her stress gradually becomes less and less. Eventually she notices almost no nervousness when the time comes to start her lesson.

This isn't as bad as I thought. I may just make it after all.

By returning every day to the stressful situation -- in this case, the classroom -- the teacher has learned that there is really no danger there. She has learned she **can**

cope. Now imagine what would have happened if she had followed her impulse to run away that first day. Unless she had quit her job, she would have had to go back the next day, and it would have been even harder to enter the room. But, because she stayed in the situation and saw it through, her second day was much easier than her first.

This is the idea behind reality testing. It can work with other situations that cause people stress, such as getting lost, being a little disorganized, speaking to people in authority, or making mistakes. The case studies in this lesson will show you some of the stresses our clients have been able to diminish using reality testing. But remember, the things that cause stress are highly individual. Before you try reality testing, you will need to identify the best areas for you. Ask your friends and relatives whether they have noticed any situations that seem to make you particularly agitated. Then review the stress management work you have been doing these last few weeks. Have you encountered situations where your stress has not diminished to the level you would like, no matter how hard you work at challenging your thoughts? Those might be good areas in which to try reality testing.

Before You Start

It is important to understand reality testing thoroughly before you experiment with it. There is an old joke about two men walking down a street together. Every five steps one of the men hits his head against a wall. Finally, his friend asks him why he keeps hitting his head against the wall, to which he replies, "It keeps the elephants away." "But there are no elephants in the middle of town!" his friend exclaims. "See, it works," he answers.

This is a good illustration of how avoidance can work in our lives. Many of our activities and behaviors are unnecessary and may even be stressful or damaging. Yet, we believe we have to carry them out in order to achieve certain ends. And as long as we continue these activities, we never learn that the bad things we are trying to avoid either don't happen or are not as bad as we thought.

A nurse who was a client of ours used to triple-check his reports because he was worried about making a mistake. Because he always checked the reports, he never learned that even if he made a small mistake, it was not a tragedy. Reality testing gets you to stop avoiding certain activities or events so that you can learn, firsthand, that they are not as bad as you thought. For example, when we got the nurse to stop checking his reports, he quickly realized that he made few mistakes and even when he did, he was not yelled at or did not lose his job.

One important point about reality testing is that it will be somewhat stressful to do. However, you do not learn without experiencing some degree of stress. Thus, you have to make yourself slightly stressed in the short-term in order to reduce your overall stress in the long-term. Our nurse, for example, became nervous and uptight at first when he did not allow himself to check his reports. However, he soon became used to the idea and in the long-run, eliminating this behavior was beneficial.

Naturally, we do not want you to stress yourself too much, and we will be discussing ways of doing reality testing in a gradual manner later.

Here are some other points to remember about reality testing:

- **Stick with it.** The key to reality testing is to stay in the situation until your stress level begins to come down. You may feel like running away, especially at first. Don't give in! If your stress becomes truly unbearable, it is okay to back away a little until you feel calmer. But try to return to the situation as soon as you can. It is like the cliche about falling off a horse; the only way to learn how to ride is to get right back on.

- **Keep practicing.** The success of reality testing is like the success of any skill or technique you have learned, it depends on practice. A stressful situation may become easier after a single session of reality testing, but it may still be difficult for you. You will need to do it again, and again, and again before it becomes easy.

- **Remember the good days.** Reality testing does not always proceed as smoothly as it did for the teacher in our earlier example. You are likely to encounter many ups and downs -- "good days" when you can last a long time in a stressful situation and not feel very nervous and "bad days" when the slightest exposure to the situation makes you want to scream. It's important not to get upset about the bad days. Everyone has them. Just do as much as you can, and get back into it again the next day. With repeated practice, your stress level **will** decrease.

- **Stay in control.** Some people who hear about reality testing do not believe it could possibly work. "I'm in that situation a lot," they say, "and it still makes me stressed -- so what good does practice do?" In reality testing, the key is that you have to deliberately put yourself into the stressful situation, as part of a gradual process of exposure. It may not always work with situations that you have to be in anyway, such as work, unless you are able to view the situation as an opportunity to practice. When you enter a situation deliberately, out of a desire to reduce your stress, you proceed much more gradually and will feel more in control. You are doing it because you want to and not because you have to. So, even if you do something unintentionally as part of your daily life, it may still help to do it intentionally as part of reality testing.

- **Beware of avoidance.** Running away from a stressful situation may not be the only way of avoiding it. There are many more subtle ways -- listening to music, taking an alcoholic drink, sitting a certain way, thinking about something else -- that you may be tempted to do to avoid dealing with the situation fully. The more aware of these techniques you are, the better your chances of stopping them. If you go into a stressful situation but deliberately do it in a way that makes it easy for you, you will not get the full benefit of reality testing.

This is not to say that you should not use these techniques at all in the beginning to make reality testing a little easier. But you should be aware of what you are doing so that eventually you can eliminate these behaviors. Remember, some degree of short-term stress is necessary for you to learn. Say that you have been working up to giving a speech, something that has always caused you a lot of stress. If you take a stiff drink of alcohol before giving the speech, you have defeated the purpose. Instead of learning that you **can** give a speech you have learned to cope by having a drink.

The same goes for such distractions as listening to music or reading. For example, if you are afraid of going into a restaurant alone but feel comfortable only when you are reading, you will not learn to reduce your stress if you force yourself to walk into the restaurant, sit down, and begin reading. In a way, you are cheating -- you may be exposing yourself to the situation physically, but not mentally.

- **Make a rule for yourself: Don't be distracted.** Instead, focus on the situation and challenge your thoughts about it, using the realistic thinking techniques. Only you know what makes you stressed and what makes it easier; only you know when you are being honest about reality testing. And, after all, only you are going to benefit from trying this technique.

Making A Stepladder

When you use reality testing, you are aiming to try things that make you nervous and not things that are too difficult. If you start by immediately throwing yourself into the most stressful situation you can imagine, you may not handle it very well. This may discourage you from trying again. We recommend you make your testing easier and more systematic by setting up a plan. We call this plan the stepladder.

To form your own stepladder, choose a stress-causing event that you want to work on. To continue an example we started earlier, let's say that you feel stress when you have to give a speech. Now think of 8 or 10 situations in which you might have to give a speech where you may feel stressed. Arrange these situations in order of their difficulty, so that number one is the easiest and the highest number is the hardest. The easiest steps go at the bottom of the ladder. It is generally best to use real-life examples if possible, but if you cannot think of an instance in which a real speech would be relatively easy to give, invent some exercises for yourself -- such as giving a speech to yourself in front of a video camera or to family or friends. Make each of these steps just a bit harder than the last one. As you complete each step, you will gain confidence to proceed to the next rung of the ladder.

Once you have completed the stepladder, think about doing the first step. You should feel a little nervous, but not overwhelmed by the idea of attempting it. If you do feel overwhelmed, break the first item down into smaller steps. Using our example, if you felt overwhelmed by the idea of giving a long speech to your spouse, you could try writing a long speech and asking your spouse to read it.

Go to Toastmasters and give unprepared speech

Go to Toastmasters and give prepared speech

Be Master of Ceremonies at friend's wedding

Give longer speech in work situation

Give brief presentation to small group

Give brief speech to friends

Give long speech to family

Give long speech to spouse

Once you became relatively comfortable with this step, you could try reading the same speech into a tape recorder and asking your spouse to listen to it. There's always a smaller, less stressful step to your larger goal.

Let's say, however, that the first step seems manageable -- not easy, but manageable to you. Then you will want to pick a time to try it out -- the sooner, the better. The longer you wait, the more time you have to worry about it. Be sure to use your realistic thinking skills here too, they will help to reduce your anxiety as much as possible beforehand. It may help if you commit yourself to a date for beginning the practice and tell someone about it, or at least write it down on your recording forms. You may ask, "How long does it take to test each step?" The answer is, "Until you become relatively comfortable (a stress level of one or two) doing it."

Remember, you are practicing the skill of coping with a stressful situation. You would not expect yourself to play a flawless piece -- or even a flawless scale -- the first time you sat down at the piano. It might take a week of practice to master a simple scale. Try not to expect more of yourself in this situation than you would if you were learning to play the piano for the first time. As you go along, you may find that the next step is too easy, or too hard. It's too easy if you can do it with no stress the first time out. In this case, just move on to the next step, or change it to make it more challenging. It's too hard if you find yourself dreading it or postponing it. In this case, break it down into easier steps.

Just follow the instructions above for making a step easier. If you have difficulty coming up with ideas, ask someone you trust for suggestions. Finally, how can you expect to feel along the way? Imagine you have just started an exercise program using a stationary bicycle. Your goal is to cycle for 30 minutes, three times a week. If you were to start out with 30 minutes, you may become discouraged quickly and quit. Even five minutes of cycling could be challenging the first week, and you might catch yourself saying, "What good is five minutes? I'll never work up to 30 minutes."

But if you keep at it, you reach a day when 5 minutes is too easy, and you decide to increase your time to 10 minutes. Ten minutes is challenging at first, but now you also feel a sense of accomplishment, both because you can see your improvement and because you stuck with it. After a few months, you reach your goal of 30 minutes, three times a week. Reality testing works the same way. At each step along the way, you will feel a mixture of challenge and accomplishment. The records you keep will demonstrate your improvement.

Reality testing was first used to help people overcome phobias, or extreme fears. Although the technique is also useful for overcoming stress, it is harder to identify stress-causing situations than it is to identify phobias. You should make a separate stepladder for each situation you want to work on. If you are having trouble identifying the steps or understanding how to proceed, the examples that follow should help.

The Health-Conscious Lawyer

Julie was a 29-year-old lawyer who was married with one young child. She tried so hard to live a healthy life that her wish to do so, which started out as a positive thing, ended up causing her a lot of stress. She had always worried about getting sick, but that worry became much worse after the birth of her son. Because of this worry, Julie went to an exercise class three times a week, tried to always eat a balanced diet, and to get a full night's sleep. Whenever she could not achieve any of these goals, she became nervous and irritable. Julie would leave parties early in order to get to bed on time. She refused to go to "unhealthy" restaurants, even if a group of friends invited her along. She became angry when the demands of family or work made her miss an exercise class.

Gradually, she realized that she had also begun to avoid other situations she considered unhealthy, such as visiting a friend in the hospital, going to a smoky bar, or even using a public restroom. Julie tried using realistic thinking techniques to reduce her worries about getting sick, but even though she realized the probability was quite low that she would become seriously ill if she missed an aerobics class, her stress level was still high.

She even tried prediction testing when she was forced to miss a class, and although she did not become ill, she continued to feel upset and angry about it. She decided it was time to take control of the situation, because she felt she had to maintain her standards whether she wanted to or not.

First, she wrote down seven situations or activities that made her nervous just thinking about them. She knew these would improve her life overall, freeing up her time and getting her out with her friends, if she could just get through them. Next she put them in order, from the easiest to the hardest, based on how stressed it made her feel to think about them. Then Julie decided to deliberately miss her aerobics class.

As the time of the class grew closer, she felt more and more stressed, but less than she had expected. Once the time for the class had passed, she was surprised to find that she felt a little relieved, and she decided to try missing the class again.

The following week, her stress level again rose as the time of the class approached, but not as much as it had the first time. By the third week, she felt very little stress when class time rolled around, and she knew she was ready to try the next step on her ladder.

As a reward that week, Julie used the time she would have spent in aerobics to play with her son, confident that she was not just distracting herself from her stress now.

Julie's Stepladder

Miss whole week of aerobics

Visit friend in the hospital

Use public restroom at restaurant

Eat fried, high fat food in restaurant

Sit in smoking section of restaurant

Go to bed two hours past bedtime

Skip one aerobics class

Note: The idea was not to encourage Julie to live an unhealthy life, but to teach her that occasionally "slipping" was not an absolute tragedy.

Similarly, the first time she stayed up two hours past her bedtime, she planned it in advance. She allowed herself to experience the worry she felt about getting sick as a result. The second time, Julie was enjoying a book she was reading so much that she spontaneously decided to stay up. Again, she felt a moderate amount of discomfort, and knew she should practice this step again.

When she did, she discovered that her stress was gone, and she felt in charge of deciding when she wanted to go to bed. She still preferred to get plenty of sleep on work nights, but she became more flexible on weekends, and when circumstances prevented her from going to bed on time, this no longer added to her stress.

After 12 weeks of reality testing, when Julie found that her concerns for her health were occupying less and less of her time, she tried her hardest test: missing a whole week of aerobics. Because she had practiced missing her Monday class, she did not feel particularly stressed over missing it this time. But when the time came for her to skip the next class, on Wednesday, her stress level increased and she felt agitated. The same thing happened on Friday, but at the same time she realized, "It's been four years since I've missed a whole week of aerobics, and I feel pretty good. We could go on vacation for a week and I wouldn't even worry about it."

When she returned to her class the following week, she was surprised at how much she really enjoyed it; something she had not felt so much when she forced herself to go religiously. Her attitude about attending the class had changed. She found herself thinking, "I hope I can get to my class on Wednesday, but if I can't, I'll just go the next time." In other words, Julie still preferred a healthy lifestyle, but she spent a lot less time worrying about it.

The Overpunctual Businessman

Peter, a 53-year-old manager, was very concerned about being on time for every appointment. If there was even a chance he would be late for something, he became stressed and irritable. As a result, he often arrived early for appointments and then wasted time waiting. If his family or co-workers were late, he became very angry at them. Peter realized that his concern with promptness was making him unhappy and hurting his relationships with other people. Peter made a stepladder, part of which is shown here.

At first, simply taking a longer route to work in the morning was almost impossible for him; he was so nervous about arriving at work late that he could barely pay attention to the road.

Gradually he realized that he usually arrived at work on time anyway, even though he had left the house later and taken a longer route. He also realized that when this new route caused him to be late, nothing happened. No one said anything, he still got his work done, and he did not waste time fuming while he waited for his co-workers to arrive.

Gradually, proceeding through the steps on his ladder, Peter learned not to become stressed when he could not avoid being late. We knew Peter had made progress when he showed up for his session one day smiling -- and 10 minutes late!

Peter's Stepladder

Arrive 10 minutes later for business meeting

Leave 10 minutes later for airport

Turn up 5 minutes later for lunch with client

Leave 5 minutes later for the theater

Turn up 5 minutes late to lunch with friends

Take long route to work in morning

Hit snooze button and sleep 10 more minutes

The Perfectionist Housekeeper

Sue, a 32-year-old secretary who had recently married, worried a lot about keeping her house perfectly clean in case guests dropped by. When she came home from a stressful day at work, she could not relax; if anything looked even slightly messy in the house, she had to tidy it up immediately. She would wash a dish as soon as anyone used it, no matter how late it was. She would make her bed every morning, even if she was running late for work. If she did not have time to clean up some mess before she left, she worried about it for the rest of the day. In addition, Sue realized that she had begun to yell at her husband every time he left something lying around.

Part of Sue's stepladder for dealing with this stress is shown here. Proceeding through the reality testing did not change the fact that Sue preferred to keep the house neat. It simply helped her to feel less stressed when circumstances prevented her from cleaning perfectly.

Sue's Stepladder

Leave dirty dishes on table all day

Leave dirty dishes on table for one hour

Leave unfolded laundry on sofa all day

Leave bed unmade all day

Leave unfolded laundry on sofa one hour

Leave unwashed dishes in sink half day

Don't tidy bathroom after husband

The Shy Cook

Sam, a 33-year-old cook, was single and preferred to work in restaurants where he was the only cook. He described himself as quiet and said he had trouble meeting new people. Although he had a few close friends and was very close to his family, Sam wanted a more active social life. In trying to make a stepladder, Sam began to realize that he was avoiding many situations that would require him to mix with other people.

For example, he would sit in the back of the bus so that he would not have to talk to the driver. He would stand rather than take a seat next to someone. He shopped in large supermarkets and department stores so that he would not have to talk to anyone in smaller shops, and he would invent excuses whenever he was invited to a party. It was a long haul from talking to the newsdealer to approaching a woman at a party, but Sam gained confidence from all the steps along the way.

Sam's Stepladder

Go to bar and talk to two new women

Go to party and talk to three new people

Buy gift in small shop and talk to salesperson

Sit beside female on bus and make small talk

Sit beside female stranger on bus

Sit beside male stranger on bus

Talk for two minutes to newsdealer

Taking Control

At this point you may be asking yourself, "Why would I want to put myself in situations that will cause me more stress, when I already have so much stress in my life? I've done a pretty good job of avoiding them up to now." There are two reasons. First, life has a way of thrusting situations upon us whether we are ready for them or not. Even if you have successfully avoided them up to now, one of these situations might come up that you can't, or don't want to avoid.

Let's say, for example, that you are nervous about speaking in public, and your sister asks you to speak at her wedding. This may be something you really want to do, but your impulse is to say no, because you are afraid you cannot cope with the stress. What if, instead, you had decided to work on this situation beforehand? You could have controlled your level of exposure to public speaking, increasing it in small steps, mastering each step until you felt comfortable with it. Then, when your sister asked, you would have been prepared to say yes -- with a little nervousness perhaps, but with a real sense of pride and accomplishment as well.

The second reason is that being a perfectionist -- whether it comes to being on time, keeping your house clean, maintaining healthy habits -- may be interfering with your life by creating more stress. You become upset every time things are not perfect, or your desire for perfection causes unnecessary conflicts with other people, or you tire yourself out trying to keep up with unrealistic standards. This is usually because you are making unrealistic predictions about the consequences of not being perfectly punctual, neat, or healthy. By deliberately testing out the reality of these predictions, you free yourself to do things because you want to, not because you have to.

The main difference between reality testing and prediction testing is that in reality testing, you arrange situations for yourself that make you feel a little stressed and practice coping with them, instead of waiting for them to come up on their own. You take control of reducing the stress in your life, instead of worrying that a particular situation might come up in the future and wondering how you will deal with it.

Lesson Summary

In this lesson we have shown you the steps to "testing reality." Admittedly, this is not always easy to do, but with practice you will do fine. Persistence and practice are important to help you develop the skill of putting yourself into uncomfortable and stressful situations. We introduced the stepladder approach that is designed to allow you to prioritize by degree of stress, situations that will help you overcome stress-causing events. Remember Sue and her aerobics class and Peter the punctual. Planning for stress will make the unavoidable stressful events less stressful and more manageable.

Assignment for Lesson 8

Over the next few weeks, you should begin to intentionally expose yourself to situations and events that cause you to become stressed. The first step is to think generally about the types of events that cause this reaction in you. Next, for each type of event, create a stepladder of situations that you can use to make a gradual approach.

Following the examples you have seen in this lesson, start with the easiest assignments and work up to the more difficult ones. Then, beginning with the easiest step, plan when, where, and how you will perform it. On page 79 is a stepladder for you to use in this assignment.

For example, if, like Peter, you worry too much about being late, you could decide to arrive five minutes late tomorrow when you pick your spouse up from work. The trick is to actually do it when tomorrow comes. This may be difficult, but it is important that you do the best you can. If you find that the step you have planned is just too stressful, at least try to do something close to it.

Make yourself be two minutes late if you can't stand to be five minutes late, and the next day work up to three minutes, etc. Obviously, you should not discuss this with your spouse ahead of time. If you do, it will not be a challenge. However, you may want to discuss it afterwards to get his or her reaction and make sure there are no hard feelings. If you are finding it difficult to get started with your first step, you may want to reread the introduction to the book, where we talked about motivation.

The final step is repetition. Keep doing the same step, or a similar one, over and over until you can do it with little stress. Once you feel comfortable with that step, move on to the next one, and keep repeating that until your stress diminishes. As you have seen by now with the other techniques you have tried, keeping records helps you measure your progress.

We now introduce the Reality Testing Practice Form. The form below shows how a completed form might look when filled out to show a particular stepladder (in this case, Julie's). Make sure that when you write down the task (the step in the step ladder) in the first column of the form, you record it very specifically. That way, it is much harder to "cheat," and much easier to tell whether you have done exactly what you set out to do.

Julie's Reality Testing Practice Form			
Task (from stepladder)	Date/Time	Expected Stress (0-8)	Actual Stress (0-8)
Skip one aerobics class	2-10 6:00 pm	7	5
Skip one aerobics class	2-17 6:00 pm	5	4
Skip one aerobics class	2-24 6:00 pm	4	1
Go to bed 2 hrs. late	2-28 10:00 pm	5	2
Go to bed 2 hrs. late	3-1 10:00 pm	4	2
Go to bed 2 hrs. late	3-5 10:00 pm	3	0
Sit in smoking section	3-6 7:00 pm	7	4
Eat high-fat food in restaurant	3-13 6:00 pm	6	3

Next, record in the second column the date and time when you plan to do the task. Before you actually try it, record in the third column the amount of stress you expect to experience. Then, after you have tried this first step on the stepladder, record in the last column the maximum amount of stress you actually experienced.

Keep practicing until you get the number in the final column down as low as you think it can go. Then move on to the next steps on your stepladder. Make a new form as you start each step, and keep repeating each step until you can do it with very little stress On page 78 we have prepared a Reality Testing Practice Form for you to copy and use.

Lesson 8 Exercise

Please answer each question by circling either true or false.

41.   Because it is aimed at reversing your tendency to avoid or escape
      situations, reality testing focuses on the behavioral system.   *True*   *False*

42.   You must stay in the stressful situation long enough for your
      stress level to decrease for reality testing to be accurate.   *True*   *False*

43.   Doing reality testing because you have to, instead of because you
      want to, does not make much difference so long as it is done.   *True*   *False*

44.   The situations that you indicate as stressful should be first on
      your stepladder.   *True*   *False*

Please turn to Appendix B on page 119 for answers to this exercise.

Reality Testing Practice Form			
Task (from stepladder)	Date/Time	Expected Stress (0-8)	Actual Stress (0-8)

My Stepladder

Specialized Techniques

The last three steps to stress management are specialized techniques involving time management, problem solving, and assertiveness. Not everyone who feels stressed will need to make changes in all these areas. But before you say to yourself, "I manage my time efficiently," or "I already know how to solve problems -- it's just that the problems in my life don't have solutions," give these lessons and exercises a try. You may be surprised at the results!

The greatest benefit from using these advanced techniques will come after you have achieved some degree of mastery using the basic skills of realistic thinking, relaxation, and reality testing. These skills are integral to applying the advanced techniques, because they will allow you to reduce your stress before you try a technique, such as assertiveness, and to realistically evaluate the results of your attempts at, say, problem solving. We have indicated the points at which you should be careful to remember to use your basic skills in each lesson.

Does your time seem to fly away from you?

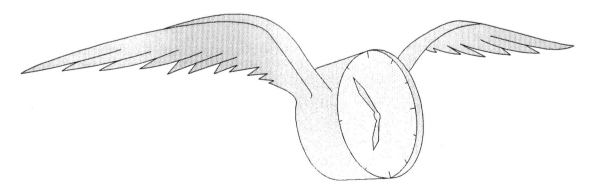

I'VE GOT TO GIVE A 5-MINUTE ORAL REPORT IN SCHOOL ON THURSDAY.

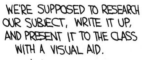

WE'RE SUPPOSED TO RESEARCH OUR SUBJECT, WRITE IT UP, AND PRESENT IT TO THE CLASS WITH A VISUAL AID.

THAT'S A BIG ASSIGNMENT.

I'LL SAY. I HATE MY TEACHER.

SHE KNOWS WE'LL ALL DO IT ON THE LAST EVENING, BUT SHE GAVE US THREE DAYS TO WORRY ABOUT IT.

Managing Your Time

Taking On Too Much

For many people, stress is either caused by or aggravated by time pressure, the feeling that there is too much to do in a day. To help you understand this pressure, consider the case of Gary, who ran a family clothing company that employed 12 people. The company's business had been increasing rapidly, which made Gary happy but also caused him more stress. As the amount of work to be done grew, Gary took on more and more responsibility; he didn't trust anyone else to do it properly.

Soon, he had so many tasks to do that he did not know where to begin. Some days he spent far too much time doing unimportant things, and other times he simply stared out the window, too overwhelmed to choose one task and start it. Though he worked longer and longer hours, he never seemed to get enough done. His relationships with friends and family suffered, he lost sleep worrying about work, and eventually he developed an ulcer.

Most of us can identify to some extent with Gary's situation. It illustrates two typical problems associated with time pressure: taking on too much and working inefficiently. Taking on more responsibilities than you can handle does not mean you are a bad worker. In fact, you probably work so well that it seems natural to try to do more and more. This is when the second problem sets in. When you have more tasks than you can perform well, you feel overwhelmed, and your ability to work efficiently suffers. You need to learn to manage your time.

Some people have no problems at all with time pressure, and if this is true for you, you may find that this lesson is not that important. However, for others, time pressure is one of the most important sources of stress, and learning to manage time is one of the most important stress management techniques. Time management is no great mystery. It simply means learning to organize and allocate your time better so that you get the most out of your day without feeling stressed.

The two main components of time management are designed to combat the two problems described above. First, you will learn **not** to overcommit yourself. Next you will learn to organize your time so that you complete your tasks efficiently and don't have to worry about forgetting things.

Which comes first, being overcommitted or being stressed? It's hard to say. People who tend to be stressed also tend to take on more than they can handle, and then, like Gary, they end up feeling even more stressed. Often this state of affairs sneaks up on you. It can be hard to say no to all the requests and opportunities that come along.

Then, before you know it, the day is over and you haven't even started the things you meant to do. As you have seen with the other stress management techniques, the first step is to become aware of what you are actually doing. To this end, you will be recording your activities for a few days so that you will have realistic evidence to act on. Before we continue, a word of warning: Time management takes time!

You may need to allow 15 or 30 minutes to record everything you do in a day. Since you are already feeling overwhelmed, it may seem silly to take on another task; you will be tempted to ignore the reporting in favor of doing something else. But remind yourself that the recording is only temporary, and it will serve an important purpose. Though it takes time now, in the long run it will save you time by reducing your stress and helping you to work more efficiently.

In other words, the time you save later will more than make up for the time you spend now. So your first step is to record everything you do for the next few days. Try not to change your schedule to make it "look better." Simply record what you are actually doing on a few of your typically busy days. Recording for three or four days should be enough; the idea is simply to get a "sample" of your typical day. You should also try to record things more than once a day so that you do not forget anything.

Recording at three or four regular intervals throughout the day should work well. We have prepared a Daily Activities Form for you to record your activities on page 85. If you have another form that will accomplish the same thing, this is fine. Use the first column to write down everything you do, even things that were unplanned and fairly brief. In the second column, record the time that you started the task and the time that you stopped. Use those times to record the duration of the task in the third column, just so it will be easier to see how much time you spent. Finally, use the last column to record any comments on the task. Was it worth doing? Did you spend too long or not long enough? Were you interrupted often? Be sure to include things like sleep, personal care, time with spouse, etc. The duration column should total to 24 hours. The chart below shows part of such a form that was completed by Gary.

Gary's Daily Activity Form

Date: March 1, 1991

Activity	Time	Duration	Comments
Work on next year's budget	9:00 - 9:30 am	30 min	Wanted to spend more time.
Phone call	9:30 - 9:40 am	10 min	
Question from Jane	9:40 - 9:45 am	5 min	She could have done it.
Thinking / daydreaming	9:45 - 10:00 am	15 min	
Phone call	10:00 - 10:05 am	5 min	
Phone call	10:05 - 10:35 am	30 min	Could have tried to cut off.
Tidy filing cabinet	10:35 - 11:00 am	25 min	Really Jane's job.
Try to design new cutter.	11:00 - 11:45 am	45 min	More important things to do
Work on next year's budget.	11:45 - 12:00 pm	15 min	Wanted to spend more time
Lunch	12:00 - 1:30 pm	90 min	Fun, but too long.

84

Daily Activity Form

Date:

Activity	Time	Duration	Comments

Once you have recorded your activities for three or four days, use the forms to make three lists. List the things you should have done but didn't during those days, the things you would have liked to do, and the things you did not do properly because you did not have enough time. Here is the list that Gary made. These lists will help you decide whether you are overcommitting yourself.

Deciding whether an activity has taken too long or is not necessary, is a very personal decision. Only you know what is efficient and what is not. The record of your daily activities should show you what you are doing each day so you are in a position to make such decisions. Sometimes it helps to get an outside perspective on your day by discussing the list with a friend or relative. On page 94 is a blank list for you to copy. The case of Carol will show you how to use these lists and forms.

Gary's Priority List

Things I should have done
Write ad for new employee

Read Sally's report on production

Cut off unnecessary phone call sooner

Things I would have liked to do
Go to get my haircut

Read Financial Review articles

Talk to Steve about his review next week

Things I didn't do well enough
Work on budget

Too long at lunch

Answer questions from Jane that she could have handled

The "Wonder Mom"

Carol was a 43-year-old mother of three who had left her part-time sales job in order to enjoy life more. After she quit, however, she found that she was feeling just as busy and stressed as she had when she was working. She couldn't understand why. Carol wrote down everything she did for three days, and she made lists of all the things she had not done or did not do very well. When she studied these forms, she was surprised at what she saw.

Carol realized that she was spending hours, doing things she didn't really need to do. Her records showed she spent nearly four hours a day preparing and serving food -- much more than she ever would have guessed. In addition, she spent over an hour each day driving her children places, even though they had managed perfectly well by themselves when she was working. Finally, her husband had started asking her to do more errands since she quit her job, and she was spending at least half an hour a day doing those.

When she listed the things she would like to do, the list included reading, working in the garden, and joining a tennis group. Reading over your lists should lead you to some new realizations. How to act on those realizations is an individual decision. Some people like full days, when they are constantly on the go, while others need more "down time," to read, think, or just relax. If your lists are full of important tasks you have had to leave undone, then it's a pretty safe bet you are overcommitted. Even if your lists are short, you will probably notice ways in which you could use your time better.

Gary, for example, recognized two major problems with his work load after he had recorded his activities for three days. He found that he was wasting time on interruptions, that his secretary could easily screen and handle, such as phone calls and office questions. He also found that he was spending so much time on unimportant tasks that he did not have enough time for big projects. This is often true of people under stress. You keep doing the small things, the things you feel you can get done in a short time, but the big things that you are putting off begin to weigh more and more heavily upon you. Once you have recognized the problem, you can start doing something about it.

Dealing with Overcommitment

If you are overcommitted, there are four ways to cut back:

- **Delegating.** If you tend to take on too much, it may be because you believe it is easier to do a task yourself than to explain it to someone else, or because you do not think others will do the task as well as you would. After a while, however, you will find that you are spending much of your time on things that someone else could easily do. The only way out of this cycle is to ask other people to take on some of your responsibilities. Carol, for example, asked her husband to do some errands on his way home from work so that she would not have to make a special trip into town. With more complicated tasks, like those at work, you may begrudge the time it takes to show someone else the ropes. But remember, the few minutes you invest in explaining now, will save you time on every occasion in the future when that task needs doing. And if you find yourself worrying that the other person may not do the task as well as you do, remember your realistic thinking techniques. Ask yourself, "How likely is it that it won't be done properly?" And then ask, "What would really happen if the other person did it wrong?"

  To return to the example of Gary, he realized that he should not be wasting his time answering phone calls from customers who wanted to check on their orders. Knowing that his secretary was perfectly capable of handling the calls and passing along to him only the customers who had problems, he decided to ask his secretary to take over this responsibility. This, as it turned out, was easier said than done. When Gary analyzed his reluctance to delegate responsibility to his secretary, he realized that he was worried she would not give the customers accurate information. So he began challenging his thoughts. What was the probability that his secretary would give customers inaccurate information? Thinking realistically, Gary realized that his secretary understood the figures as well as he did, and it was highly unlikely that she would be wrong. But what if she was wrong? What would really happen if she made a mistake? After some thought, Gary realized that most of his customers would be understanding if she made a mistake -- and, if any were not, he would be right there to step in. So by applying realistic thinking to time management, Gary was able to reduce his work load significantly.

- **Saying no.** Many people run out of time because they spend so much of their day doing things they do not want to do -- taking on the work of less efficient employees, for example, or talking to people who just will not go away. Being assertive is very important in limiting how much you do in a day. We will discuss assertiveness in more detail in Lesson 11. For now, though, just remind yourself that people will not be angry at you or hate you just because you do not have time to do something for them. If you can make yourself say no, once or twice a day, you will find that you have a lot more time.

Carol, for example, found that she could give herself more time by not automatically agreeing to take her children everywhere they wanted to go. Although they were annoyed at first, within a few weeks they did not ask for rides unless they really needed them, yet they still found ways to get around. Similarly, she asked her husband to do some of his own errands.

After a few weeks, Carol asked her family how they felt about these changes. To her surprise, they said that they realized they had been placing too many demands on her, and they didn't mind the changes at all.

Mom's Taxi Service

Don't Let Your Family "Schedule" All of Your Time

- **Sticking to agendas.**
Another reason that some people run out of time is that they do a task in an inefficient way, or they start one task and end up doing several others. As an example of the first problem, let's say you have gotten into the habit of going out to lunch with a colleague every time you have an issue to discuss. If you want to go to lunch because it is fun or relaxing, that's fine. But if you are doing it simply to discuss business, then it may be far more efficient to write a memo or talk on the phone.

Now, what needs to be done first?

Examples of the second problem are easy to find. Let's say you have decided to make more space in your attic by restacking some boxes. But once you get up there, you start opening all the boxes and reading old letters, looking at old photos, etc. It is important that when you set out to do a particular task, you do that task -- and **ONLY** that task -- quickly and efficiently. If other tasks arise as a result of the first, think of them as separate jobs that need to be scheduled into a time of their own.

- **Assessing priorities.** Perhaps the most important thing you must do once you realize you are overcommitted is to convince yourself that some things simply are not going to get done. You need to set priorities -- in the short-term, by deciding what to do each day, and in the long-term, by deciding how you want to live your life.

One of our clients, for example, was working three jobs and trying to raise two children. As a result, she was feeling very stressed because she did not think she was giving the children enough attention. After recording her activities and thinking about how she spent her time, she decided that the extra money she earned from her third job was less important than spending more time with her children. So she quit that job.

For some people, giving up a task creates stresses all on its own. If this is true for you, go back to the realistic thinking strategies and use them as we have shown in this lesson. Assessing priorities and organizing are so important that we will discuss them in more detail in the following section.

Labeling and Scheduling

Once you have examined your typical day, the next step is to assign each task a priority and work out a schedule so that the important things get done. It's easiest to start this by planning just one day -- say, tomorrow. Make a list of all the things you plan to do tomorrow. Then go through the list and label the tasks according to how important they are: **A tasks, B tasks,** or **C tasks.** We will explain what those labels mean on the next page.

- **A tasks** are top priority. Give an A only to tasks that absolutely, positively have to be done that day. Some days you may have no A tasks, while other days you may have several. Be strict with the label. Ask yourself, "Do I really have to do this today?" If not, it is not an A task.

- **B tasks** are the most common type -- things that are important but do not necessarily have to be done immediately. Of course, if they are not done, B tasks will eventually become A tasks. You should not feel stressed if you cannot get to a B task immediately. But do try to do it before it becomes an A task, to keep stress at a minimum.

- **C tasks** are those that will need to be done someday, but at the moment they are not too important. Some C tasks can stay C tasks indefinitely, while others will eventually become B or even A tasks. Once you have divided up your tasks this way, the next step is to organize them. Use a recording sheet like the Daily Planner on page 90.

First, write on the sheet all the tasks that must be done at a specific time, such as attending a meeting, picking up your children, or having lunch with a client. Then, beginning with the A tasks, write the other tasks into time slots when you think you can do them. Do not schedule all the A tasks together. Instead, follow an A task with a B or C task. That way, if something keeps you from doing the A task, you can reschedule the B or C task and still get the A task done.

The chart below shows a sample of Carol's Daily Planner. On this day, Carol had two A tasks: taking her daughter to the dentist and meeting with the builder who was helping Carol and her husband plan an addition to their home. She originally wanted to list cooking dinner as an A task, but she realized that the family could eat leftovers or get takeout food, which her kids considered a treat. Carol's B tasks on this day were grocery shopping, cooking dinner, and playing tennis with a friend. Her C tasks were working in the garden, reading, and studying for her language class.

Carol's Daily Planner			
Time	**Task**	**Rating (A, B, C)**	**Done? (Check)**
9- 10 am	Work in garden	C	
10- 11 am	Meet with builder	A	
11- 12 pm	Shopping	B	
12- 1 pm	Lunch and read	C	
1- 3 pm	Tennis	B	
3- 4 pm	Dentist	A	
4- 5 pm	Cook dinner	B	
5- 6 pm	Study	C	

Daily Planner			
Time	Task	Rating (A, B, C)	Done? (Check)

She realized that studying for her language class, which met in three days, would move from a C, to a B, and then to an A task as the day of the class approached. Similarly, because grocery shopping, now a B task, would become an A task soon, she decided to get it done. Since it was a task she disliked, she scheduled herself a reward: time to read when she returned from shopping.

Flexibility And Rewards

Carol's daily plan illustrates two important factors you should consider in making your own: staying flexible and "reward" yourself. Making a daily plan is supposed to reduce your stress, not increase it. If you schedule your tasks so tightly that any interruption throws the whole schedule off, then you may not be able to stick to the schedule and may feel even more stressed. If you put all of the unpleasant tasks together, both your efficiency and your mood may soon suffer.

When you are scheduling your tasks, especially the most important ones, estimate how long the task will take and then **double** that time. Tasks almost always take longer than you expect. You are bound to run into unexpected hitches, interruptions, or emergencies that distract you. So give yourself plenty of time.

You will be surprised at how much you can get done in a day when you organize it logically, even if you allow a lot of time for each task. And would you agree that it is better to end your day with three completed tasks than six half-finished ones?

Approach the scheduling realistically; plan for how your day really goes, not how you wish it would go. That means allowing for any time-consuming events that are likely to happen, whether you like them or not.

For example, one of our clients owned several apartment buildings and was constantly being called to come and make repairs. She did not enjoy this, but she knew it would keep happening. When she made her daily plan, she scheduled two hours a day for such calls and repairs.

Carol's Priority List

Things I should have done

Mail out that package to Mom

Finish the laundry

Work on the kids' Easter outfits

Take the dog to the vet

Things I would have liked to do

Work in the garden

Play tennis

Finish that book I'm reading

Sit down with the kids

Things I didn't do well enough

Return those library books on time

Fixing dinner took too long

Schedule some study time

Allow more time for grocery shopping

That way, if she needed more than two hours to do the work, she could put off some B or C task to get it done. But if she received no repair calls one day, she would have two spare hours to use as she wished. It is also important to schedule rewards -- in other words, to schedule rests or enjoyable tasks after particularly difficult jobs.

This practice gives you a break, helps you to relax, and helps to make you more efficient as you move on to the next task. Often, C tasks are more fun than A or B tasks; you can use them as rewards, as Carol did. A different type of reward is to look over your planning sheet at the end of the day and check off all the tasks you completed. Chances are, you will end up with a strong feeling of accomplishment.

Lesson Summary

In this lesson we have shown you the importance of managing your time. Taking on too many tasks and managing them inefficiently can be a leading cause of stress for many people. Even if you believe that you manage your time efficiently, you should follow our suggestions in this lesson; you **will** be amazed at what you discover. You now have some tips on how to deal with overcommitments. Delegating, saying no, sticking to an agenda, and assessing priorities can all help to reduce your daily stress level. Labeling your tasks on a scale of A-C can not only help you prioritize your tasks, it can add to your self-esteem when you see how much you "really" do accomplish.

Assignment for Lesson 9

Your assignment for this week is first to record your daily activities and list the other things you want to get done for three or four days. Once you have decided on any changes you may want to make in the way that you run your days, you should begin to make daily plans and organize your tasks according to priorities.

It is generally best to allow five minutes each morning to plan what you will do that day, although some people prefer to plan their next day the previous night. Some people find that planning their days for one or two weeks is enough to give them an idea of the sorts of difficulties they need to watch out for. They may then stop planning in a formal fashion but may go back to structured planning if their schedules become very busy or they begin feeling tense. For others, formal planning of the day is an excellent way to reduce stress. These people may make a brief plan of their day, every day, for the rest of their lives.

Some people find that their days are so unpredictable that actually making a plan is restrictive or impractical. If that is true of you, you can do a modified version. Divide your tasks into levels of importance and then write a list of tasks you would like to get done that day. If you cannot schedule them by time, just list them in order of importance: most important tasks at the top of the page, down to the least important tasks at the bottom. Include a generous estimate of how much time you think each task will take.

When you find yourself with some free time in your unpredictable schedule during the day, you can pull out your list and start doing your tasks, beginning with the top one. Cross off each task as you do it so that you can see what you have accomplished. Whether your days lend themselves to a strict daily plan or not, it is a good idea to keep track of one more thing. Jot down all the unplanned tasks you did during the day. That way, if you get to the end of the day and find that you did not complete many of the tasks on your original list, you will know that you still accomplished something.

"All this sounds great," you say. "But it would never work for my schedule. My husband does not have time to run his own errands," or "My secretary really can't handle the phone calls herself; we've tried." It is important to realize that you will not be able to delegate all of the tasks you dislike, or that waste your time. But there may be a more efficient way to do them. Perhaps your husband can give you a list of errands for the week and you can do them in a block, instead of making several trips. Maybe your secretary can take messages so that you have some uninterrupted work time, and you can return these calls at a certain time during the day.

In the next lesson we will show you a way to generate solutions to problems like these. If you find yourself making schedules and not sticking to them, chances are you may still be trying to do too much, or you have not recognized your true priorities. Keep working at it until you come up with a schedule you can live with. You will know you have found it by the reduction in your level of stress.

Lesson 9 Exercise

Please answer each question by circling either true or false.

45. You can accomplish more in a day if you overcommit yourself to too many tasks because you will do each faster.   *True*   *False*

46. To be assertive with your time is to limit unnecessary and unimportant activities and interruptions.   *True*   *False*

47. It is better to tackle tasks as each arises versus putting them off until a later time.   *True*   *False*

48. "B" tasks are important and are completed the same day.   *True*   *False*

49. You should first estimate the time required to finish a task and then double that time.   *True*   *False*

Please turn to Appendix B on page 119 for answers to this exercise.

My Priority List

Things I should have done

_____

_____

_____

_____

_____

Things I would have liked to do

_____

_____

_____

_____

_____

Things I didn't do well enough

_____

_____

_____

_____

_____

Solving Real Problems

Sometimes stress is caused by exaggerated worries that lend themselves well to realistic thinking and challenging your thoughts. But sometimes you have problems that are not exaggerated; they are difficult, and you really cannot think of a solution. Problems like these, for which the right course of action is not always clear, can greatly increase your stress. You may find yourself lying awake at night thinking about these problems, or having trouble concentrating at work because of all the issues on your mind.

You need a way to deal with these problems. The following technique should help when you have trouble thinking of a solution to a problem. The technique is very simple and makes common sense. It is also effective.

Basically, it is an extension of realistic thinking, which you are already good at. The technique addresses the two things that happen when you face a difficult problem: you feel too overwhelmed to define the problem clearly, and you feel that no possible solution exists. Let's look at these two issues separately.

Defining The Problem

It is difficult to believe at first, but even when you are feeling so overwhelmed by a problem that you seem to think about nothing else, you may not be seeing the problem clearly. People tend to think of their problems in very broad, vague ways that assume the worst. So your first task will be to think through the specific, objective details of the problem. In other words, ask yourself, "What exactly is the problem here?" As usual, writing out your thoughts can help you organize them.

The Problem Solving Form on page 100 may be helpful for you to write out your thoughts. In the first column, write exactly what the problem is. This may take some thought. You want specific details, not vague descriptions. And you want the actual, objective problem, not your feelings about it.

Let's say, for example, that you are having trouble with employees who are not showing up regularly for work. You could write, "Employees not showing up for work," but that is vague. You could write, "Stupid employees care nothing about their jobs," -- but that, obviously, is a bit emotional! It is also catastrophizing, or assuming the worst possible motive. Instead, a good practical description of the problem might read like this: "Two employees (Mark and Jan) did not come in to work on two days this week."

Problems are not always what they seem on the surface. But you cannot solve them until you find out what they really are. In other words, you must find the cause or root of the problem. For example, if your child is not doing well in school, there could be any number of solutions, depending on what is causing the problem. In this case, defining the problem as "Johnny is not doing well at school," would not be nearly as useful as stating, "Johnny's school is not teaching properly," or "Johnny is not interested in school work."

Defining the problem specifically is critical in helping you find a solution. Take some time to think about what is really at the root of the problem. Sometimes you can think and think and still not know the cause of a problem. Then that becomes your problem, and you can apply the problem-solving technique to this issue first. In other words, in the problem column you could write, "Not knowing why Johnny is doing poorly at school." When you move on to the next step of the technique, coming up with solutions, all your solutions will be aimed at trying to find out why Johnny is not doing well. Once you know that, you can work on a solution to that problem.

Finding A Solution

Just as people often have trouble defining a problem, they also have trouble believing that any solution to the problem exists. But in fact, nearly every problem has a solution; sometimes it is just hard to think of it. This is when you can try what we call "brainstorming." Brainstorming means letting your mind go and writing down every possible solution to the problem, no matter how impractical or ridiculous it sounds. The idea is simply to get your mind working. When you do, you may happen upon a solution that never would have occurred to you otherwise. Therefore, anything you think of, no matter how dumb it sounds, can help by leading you to another possibility.

Let's say, for example, that your problem is that your neighbor's dog is keeping you awake at night by barking. After writing that problem in the first column of the form, you proceed to the second column and brainstorm these ideas: talking to your neighbors, asking them to sell the dog, asking them to keep the dog inside at night, and poisoning the dog. Chances are, you would not seriously consider poisoning the dog! But writing down this idea helps you vent your frustrations and may lead you to another idea, such as calling the police. Once you have written down every possible solution you can think of, decide which ones are practical (poisoning the dog may be possible, but it certainly is not responsible!). Then rank them.

Which of the practical solutions is the best? The next best? List them in order, in the final column of the sheet, until all of the practical solutions are accounted for. You can use your realistic thinking skills to help rank the solutions. For example, you could ask yourself, "How likely is this solution to work?" and "If it does not work, what could the consequences be?"

For example, your problem may be that your car is having mechanical trouble. One solution would be to buy a new car. The probability that this solution would work is 100%. The consequences would include the high cost, the great amount of time it would take, and so on. Another solution would be to have the car repaired. The probability that this solution would work may be only 80%. But the consequences might include this solution being less expensive and relatively quick. Listing probabilities and consequences can make it easier for you to decide which solution you prefer to try first.

The list in the last column now becomes your plan of action. First, you will try the solution that seems best. If that does not work, or can not be accomplished for some reason, you can move on to the next solution on the list. You should also continue to apply your realistic thinking techniques to the problem, even after you have listed the potential solutions. Sometimes when you ask yourself, "What is the worst that can happen if this problem is not resolved?", you will be surprised at how non-threatening the answer is.

A sample form and plan of action are shown below. This form was filled out by Julia, whose husband complained that she was spending too much time with her best friend. When Julia thought about the situation, she realized that the real problem was that her husband, Don, did not like her best friend, Mary. So that is what she wrote in the first column. The second column shows all the possible solutions that Julia brainstormed. You can see that some of them are sensible and practical, such as "arrange a night out with Don and Mary," while others are impractical, such as "divorce Don." After studying her brainstorming column, Julia decided that three of the solutions were practical.

Julia's Problem Solving Form

Exact Problem	Brainstorming	Plan of Action
Don doesn't like Mary	Talk to Don about Mary. Arrange night out with Don and Mary. Divorce Don. Plan separate times with Don and Mary. Stop seeing Mary. Tell off Don.	1. Arrange night out with Don and Mary. 2. Talk to Don about Mary. 3. Plan separate time with Don and Mary.

The one that appealed to her most was going out with both Don and Mary so that they could get to know each other. She listed that first in her plan of action. If that did not work, she would try talking to Don about all of Mary's good points and explaining why her friendship with Mary was important to her. And if that did not work, she would talk with her husband and see if they could set up an acceptable amount of time for her to spend with Mary. Finally, Julia applied her realistic thinking skills to the problem and asked herself what would happen if Don never learned to like Mary.

She immediately realized that she was afraid that if Don continued to dislike Mary, he would eventually dislike her, Julia, as well. Looking at that thought realistically, she quickly concluded that the probability of her husband hating her was close to zero. She realized that while she would prefer her husband to like her best friend, it was not the end of the world if he didn't.

Lesson Summary

Many of the techniques we have discussed up until now, have been focused on thinking realistically about events in your life that cause you to be stressed. By now you have become proficient at listing and assigning probabilities to the possible outcomes of certain events. Most of the time you have discovered what seemed to be a "big" problem was in fact a much "smaller" problem. There are times, however, when all of us face very large and real problems. In this lesson we have discovered that the first step to solving these problems is to identify them. Once a problem has been clearly identified, brainstorming possible solutions can help to identify solutions that are logical and practical. Listing the possible solutions, in their order of priority can then lead to a plan of action for solving the problem.

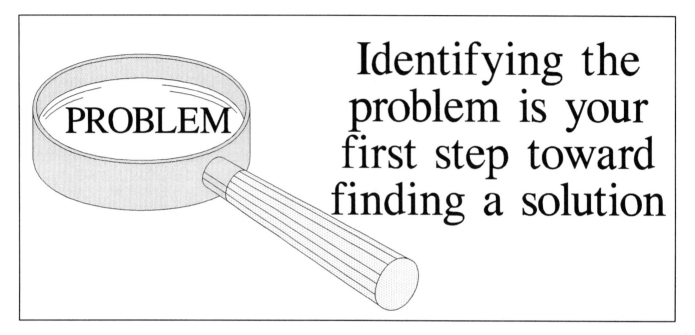

Assignment for Lesson 10

Try this technique with a problem that has been bothering you lately. Use the form on page 100. The first step is to identify the problem, taking care to specify the root cause (if you know it -- if not, back up and brainstorm possible causes). Then, brainstorm as many solutions as you can come up with. It may help to put the problem aside overnight or for a few days, and come back to it to see if other solutions occur to you. You may find, as you brainstorm, that some of your solutions are funny -- the humor will help you get a perspective on the problem.

Next, you should decide which solutions are practical and rank them in order, deciding which is the best solution, the next best, and so on. Finally, try out the first solution on your list, and evaluate the results. If you are not satisfied, go on to the next solution.

No pressing problems this week? You may still want to practice this technique, either by using your imagination and inventing a problem, by following one of the examples in this lesson (what would you do to figure out why Johnny is not doing well in school?), or by applying the problem-solving to a problem you resolved successfully in the past. Considering other solutions to a problem you have already solved can help you increase your flexibility for the future.

Lesson 10 Exercise

Please answer each question by circling either true or false.

50. The first thing to do when facing a problem is to define it in specific details.

    True   *False*

51. A common error encountered with facing a problem is the tendency to believe that there is no possible solution.

    True   *False*

52. Brainstorming refers to the idea of thinking hard for a long time for one good idea to use as a solution to a problem.

    True   *False*

53. It is not necessary to apply realistic thinking skills once you have brainstormed for solutions to a problem.

    True   *False*

Please turn to Appendix B on page 119 for answers to this exercise.

Problem Solving Form

Exact Problem	Brainstorming	Plan of Action

Asserting Yourself

See if this scene sounds familiar. A friend or co-worker asks you to do something that you really do not want to do, but you give in and agree to do it anyway. Then, later, another friend finds out and scolds you, saying, "Why in the world did you agree to that? You have got to be more assertive!" You now feel confused. Maybe you should have stood up for yourself; on the other hand, you did not want to seem pushy and selfish. You may not have asserted yourself because you thought it would cause stress, but it turns out that not asserting yourself is causing you stress, too.

Some people simply do not know how to assert themselves in any situation. These people could benefit from reading one of the many good books on assertiveness that have flooded the market in recent years, or from joining an assertiveness training group and practicing the necessary skills. Most people, however, do know how to be assertive. They just do not feel comfortable doing it, and they are never quite sure when it is the right thing to do. If you are part of this large group -- if the lack of assertiveness is not a chronic problem but simply another source of stress -- then you need to learn appropriate assertiveness. The principles discussed in this brief lesson can help.

What Is Assertiveness

Being assertive does not mean always getting your way. Rather, being assertive means developing a feel for your rights in a situation and feeling comfortable asking others to respect those rights. The key is to use assertiveness only when it is appropriate. There are times when you really should insist on having your way, even if it causes some inconvenience to someone else. But there are other times when you have to put your own needs aside because the other person's needs are even more important. The trick is to learn the difference. Realistic thinking techniques, which should be second nature to you by now, can help in this process. Two cases from our clients illustrate how the techniques work.

Karen's Date

Karen, a 19-year-old student, had been repeatedly asked on dates by Todd, a friend of her brother. Karen had no interest in dating Todd. Although she made excuses whenever he asked her out, she told us that the situation was making her uncomfortable. We asked, "What would happen if you told Todd you did not want to go out with him?" Karen replied that Todd would be hurt. But when she looked at that thought realistically, she realized that after all the times she had already said no, there was probably only a 50 percent chance that Todd would be hurt. Further, Karen realized that she had been imagining a dire consequence of Todd's being hurt. She was assuming that he would never get over it. Even more, she believed that if Todd did not get over the rejection, it would be her fault.

Thinking realistically, Karen saw that Todd probably would recover quite well if she asserted herself and told him she was not interested in dating him. And if he didn't recover, it would be Todd's responsibility, not hers. Karen was not being nasty or cruel, but was realizing that she could not be expected to take responsibility for other people's feelings. In other words, if Todd took the chance of asking her out, he had to be prepared for her to say no, and Karen could not be expected to do something she did not want to do just to keep Todd happy -- if she did, the situation might never end.

Simon's Request

Simon, a 28-year-old clerk, faced a different challenge to his assertiveness. He wanted to ask for a week off from work, only a month after he had taken a vacation, to help his father who had just come out of the hospital. Simon's initial thought was that his boss would say no. Realistically, however, he had to admit that he had no idea what his boss would say; therefore, the probability of a negative answer was probably only about 50 percent. So Simon asked himself, "What happens if my boss does say no?" His fear, he realized, was that she would consider him lazy and would fire him.

In fact, however, the evidence showed that Simon's boss had praised him in the past for his hard work. So even if she said no to the time off, she would be highly unlikely to fire him, or even to consider him lazy. Based on his realistic thinking, Simon realized that he should ask for the time off, since there was a chance he would get it, and whether he did or not, his boss would be unlikely to think badly of him or fire him. In addition, he felt that he had a right to ask for the time off since he had an important reason for his request.

Applying Other Techniques

The stress management techniques you have learned in this program form a powerful arsenal that you can apply to a variety of situations. Realistic thinking, for example, can help you understand your reluctance to assert yourself. Often, people do not practice assertiveness because they are afraid that other people may dislike them. Clearly, a person who goes around demanding his or her own way all the time is not going to be too popular! But if you use assertiveness appropriately, after weighing the pros and cons in a given situation, people will respect you for standing up for your rights. Try asking yourself such realistic thinking questions as, "How likely is it that this person will be angry at me?" and "What is the worst that can happen if I ask?"

Realistic thinking is not the only technique that applies to assertiveness. You can also try putting yourself in the other person's place, as we discussed in Lesson 7. For example, you could switch the situation in your mind and ask yourself, "If this person were to ask the same favor of me, would I be angry?" And assertiveness, like the other techniques you have tried, improves with practice. Assertiveness training groups can help, since they get you to practice assertive responses in the safety of a group, in order to build confidence. You might also want to look at assertiveness as a kind of reality testing, as we discussed in Lesson 8. Now that you know how to make a stepladder, you can make one for situations in which you find assertiveness difficult.

For example, you could put something relatively easy, like asking your spouse a favor at the bottom of the ladder, and something more difficult, like saying no to your boss, at the top. Then you could try the first situation and keep practicing it until you feel more comfortable with assertiveness. Do not forget to use your realistic thinking skills during your practices. Prediction testing, which you learned in Lesson 6, can be a particularly useful technique to combine with this sort of stepladder.

Before you try each step, make and record your predictions about what you think might happen. How do you think you will feel? How will the other person respond? Then, when you have completed the practice, make a note of whether your predictions came true. Applying familiar techniques to assertiveness in this way can help reduce one more source of stress in your life.

We will end the lesson with the example of Matt, who tried the stepladder and was surprised at the results. Matt worked as a nurse in a large hospital. Although he had started out liking his job, he knew he was not being assertive enough at work. As a result, he often got the worst shifts, had to do extra work, and got stuck with the unpleasant jobs that other people refused to do. The more this happened, the more stress Matt felt. He worked out a stepladder of assertiveness tasks to practice, part of which is shown here.

Before trying each one, he predicted what the outcome would be. For example, before asking the head nurse to assign him to an earlier shift, Matt predicted that she would say no. To his surprise, she said that she would be happy to discuss the situation and reach a compromise.

As he finished each step, Matt compared his prediction with what had actually happened, and he continued practicing each task until he could do it easily. Over the weeks, Matt began to enjoy his job more. A major source of stress in his life had been reduced. The table below shows the first few steps of the ladder for Matt's Prediction Testing.

Matt's Stepladder

Ask doctor to do rounds in certain order

Ask head nurse to change shift

Refuse to change shifts with colleague

Ask head nurse for more surgery assistance

Ask to change shifts with colleague

Refuse to help colleague with cleaning

Ask orderly to tidy up

Make small request from patient

Matt's Prediction Testing Form			
Event	**Guess**	**Test**	**Outcome**
Ask Mr. Willis in room 212 to turn his television down.	He will refuse. He will tell my supervisor.	Asked him to turn down TV. See if supervisor complains.	He agreed. He didn't complain to anyone.
Ask orderly to tidy up.	He will be angry. He will do a poor job.	Watch his face. Check supply room when he is finished.	He looked annoyed, but he was friendly later in the day. Supply room looked fine, even better than usual!

Lesson Summary

The lack of assertiveness is a major cause of stress for many people. As we discussed in Lesson 10, this can lead to overcommitment, which leads to inefficiency, which leads to poor time management, which eventually leads to more stress. Being assertive can cause a certain degree of stress itself, however, the additional stress that it saves in the long-run is the reward you are looking for. You can combine the various techniques we have discussed throughout this manual to help you in evaluating certain situations where assertiveness may or may not be appropriate. Just like the other skills you have learned through this program, being assertive takes practice.

Assignment for Lesson 11

Some people do not find asserting themselves difficult. If you are one of them, you can skip this assignment. But if assertiveness has been a problem for you, you should make a list of requests and refusals to use for practice. You may not be able to plan opportunities to refuse other people's requests, but over the next week you should try to notice when you agree to do something. Ask yourself afterward if you really want to do, and have time for, whatever you agreed to do. During the following week, try to pause before automatically agreeing to do things for other people. Once you break the habit of saying yes automatically, you can try telling people, "I'll think about whether I can do that for you, and get back to you."

This is an interim step to learning to say no when you know immediately that you do not want to, or cannot, take on the additional responsibility. Form a stepladder and begin to practice the least stressful items, just like you did when you were working on reality testing. Use all of the techniques you learned earlier for realistic thinking: estimating the likelihood and consequences of a negative outcome and testing your predictions when you practice. You may find that the people in your life are a little disappointed at first to find that they can no longer rely on you to accede to their demands. But you will also find that you resent them less for imposing on you, and you may want to reconsider relationships that seem based solely on your contributions -- acquaintances who are never able to fulfill your requests but always expect you to help them out.

Lesson 11 Exercise

Please answer each question by circling either true or false.

54. Being assertive is the act of voicing your rights and feelings to others appropriately and respectfully.   *True*   *False*

55. You do not really need your realistic thinking techniques while being assertive, for you will not have time to do them while trying to be assertive.   *True*   *False*

56. The difficulty for people in assertiveness training is in learning how to be assertive.   *True*   *False*

57. Assertive behavior does not generally reduce stress disorders, but it will make you feel better.   *True*   *False*

58. The stepladder of situations can be applied to situations in which you need to be assertive.   *True*   *False*

Please turn to Appendix B on page 119 for answers to this exercise.

And another thing . . . I want you to be more assertive! I'm tired of everyone calling you Alexander the Pretty-Good!

Facing the Future

Kick off your shoes, relax, and think about where you were before you started this program. Did stress seem like a big mystery, an ugly dragon you had to battle every day to stay in control of your life? Now think about your situation today, after months of practicing stress management techniques. Are you feeling calmer and more in control? When you feel the symptoms of stress coming on, do you find yourself thinking, "Okay, I know what this is, and I know what to do about it"? Okay! Give yourself some credit! None of us feel calm every day of our lives, but you have come a long way from the person who filled out those first forms. If you don't believe that, just look back at the forms and you will see. It is important to keep your expectations realistic -- after all, you don't want the process of mastering stress to cause you more stress! You cannot expect every one of your recording forms to show zero stress.

As we have emphasized throughout the book, having some stress in your life is not only natural but healthy. It helps keep you motivated, and it keeps your life challenging enough to be interesting. You should also remember that the skills you have been learning are designed to last a lifetime. They will never be perfect, but they will become more effective the more you practice them. By now, for example, you can probably do your relaxation at will, wherever you happen to be. Just think how different that is from the first time you sat with your eyes closed in a dark room, struggling to concentrate.

Before we send you out to a lifetime of practice, we need to make one last point: No matter how skilled you become at practicing your relaxation techniques, there will probably be times in your life when circumstances leave you feeling extremely stressed. Everyone faces major upheavals -- a loved one dying, a business failing, a family crisis coming to a head. When you face such situations, remind yourself of two very important things. First, feeling stress in trying times is natural and expected; there is a perfectly rational explanation for your response, and it's part of being human -- everyone's life is punctuated with crises. But these things pass, and no matter how bad you feel, remember too that you are better off than you would have been before, because now you possess specific skills to help keep your stress from becoming excessive or going on longer than it should.

As we have repeated throughout this book, the problem is not that you experience stress; the goal of this program is not to make you an unresponsive zombie. The problem is that you experience stress so intensely or excessively that it controls and ruins your life.

Now you know of some ways to take back control. And going back to basics and working on individual techniques is by no means an admission of defeat. The more you practice, the more success you will have. If you incorporate realistic thinking and the other exercises into your daily life, they will become so automatic that you will not even notice you are doing them. You will just notice the effect -- a calmer you. With your stress under control, you should be able to get excited about things again, and actually enjoy your job, your family, and your friends.

You are now a master of stress management, and your mastery will increase with time. So get out there and practice. You are ready to go.

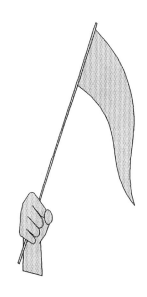

The Role of Drugs in Stress Management

If you were taking a prescription drug for stress before you started this program, you may now be ready to stop taking it -- if that's what you want to do. We have not addressed this topic before now because it was important for you to learn to master your stress before stopping your medication. About half the people who were taking medication for stress feel ready to stop taking it by the time they finish this program. Many of the others stop within a year.

This lesson will describe some of the most common drugs and give you tips for curtailing your dosage. But do not rush yourself; there is no need to stop your medication until you are ready. And remember that you should always work with your physician when making any change involving prescription drugs.

Common Drugs For Stress

The drugs most commonly prescribed for relief of short-term stress are minor tranquilizers, most of which are part of a class known as benzodiazepines. This group includes dozens of types and brand names, among them diazepam (Valium), and alprazolam (Xanax).

These drugs usually are prescribed only for short periods because people develop a tolerance for them. In other words, after a few weeks you would need more and more of the benzodiazepine to produce the same effect, and you would run the risk of becoming dependent on it. If you did develop a dependence, you would experience withdrawal symptoms when you stopped taking it.

For this reason, most doctors prescribe these minor tranquilizers only to help a patient through a difficult situation, not for long-term use. Another type of drug for stress, which is new, is called buspirone (BuSpar). Although BuSpar acts something like a benzodiazepine, it does not produce the same sort of tolerance effect. On the other hand, since it is a new drug, it has not been extensively tested for its effects on stress and anxiety.

Anti-depressants are also prescribed once in a while for stress and anxiety. Some of the more common ones include a category called tricyclic anti-depressants, which includes imipramine (brand name Tofranil) and amitriptyline (Elavil). Another category, the monoamine-oxidase (MAO) inhibitors, includes phenelzine (Nardil).

The tricyclic anti-depressants have some side effects that can seem to increase stress early in the treatment cycle, but these effects go away with time. The MAO inhibitors require diet restrictions in order to prevent such side effects as rising blood pressure. Anti-depressants can be taken for a longer time and are easier to withdraw from than the minor tranquilizers.

Stopping Your Drug Use

Now that you have a large variety of stress management techniques at your disposal, you may feel ready to stop taking your medication. Be sure to consult your doctor. Only he or she knows how quickly you can safely taper off the dosage until you no longer need medication. Because you now know so much about stress, you should have little trouble stopping your drug use if you follow these guidelines:

- **Withdraw slowly.** Despite what you may have seen in the movies, "cold turkey" is not the way to go. Ask your doctor to help you work out a schedule for diminishing your dosage.

- **Set a target date**. You and your doctor should pick a date by which you hope to be completely off drugs. This date should be far enough away to allow for gradual tapering off, but not so far away that your goal seems unreachable.

- **Use your stress management techniques.** Eliminating your medication is nothing to get stressed about! Most people can cope quite well with a gradual decrease in dosage. But some people find that their feelings of stress temporarily grow stronger as they begin withdrawing from a drug. This kind of "outbreak" of stress, which is more likely to happen if you have been taking one of the benzodiazepines, nearly always goes away after a week or two, as the drug clears out of your system. If you experience an "outbreak," simply do your relaxation and try the other techniques you have been using all along.

For example, you may think that you are having a total relapse or that your anxious feelings will never end. But how likely is that, really? You just learned that a lot of people feel this way for a few days when they stop taking their tranquilizers, but that it does go away. Also, if you have been taking a small amount of a drug for a long time, your body may have little or no reaction, but you may feel insecure about not having your pills with you. Some of our patients carry pill bottles with them for a long time without ever taking a pill. (Some people even get the same secure feeling carrying an empty bottle.)

In this case, the stressful situation you are facing is being without pills. But what do you think would happen if you went a day or two without carrying your pill bottles around? Whatever that is, how likely is it to happen? And would it be so terrible if it did? Try some reality testing on this situation. Go for a day without carrying your pill bottle -- then two days. You might be surprised by the result. Utilizing your relaxation and realistic thinking, along with other stress reduction procedures, can help you stop taking medication for stress.

In a few people, withdrawal from a benzodiazepine can cause severe anxiety or panic attacks. Your doctor can help adjust your schedule to cope with this problem.

Afterword Exercise

Please answer each question by circling either true or false.

59. The evidence is unclear whether or not certain prescribed drugs are effective for stress relief.   *True*   *False*

60. It is possible to become dependent upon benzodiazepines with prolonged use.   *True*   *False*

61. You will not experience withdrawal effects from going off prolonged use of benzodiazepines.   *True*   *False*

62. The more gradual and paced your withdrawal from medication, the better your chances of eliminating your dependency.   *True*   *False*

63. Although some people have mastered stress using the principles in this book while in the process of withdrawal from drugs, they still experience stress during withdrawal and find it very difficult to cope.   *True*   *False*

Please turn to Appendix B on page 119 for answers to this exercise.

"When I got home, Harold's coat and hat were gone, his worries were on the doorstep, and Gladys Mitchell, my neighbor, says she saw him heading west on the sunny side of the street."

Self-Assessment Exercises - Master List

Introduction Exercise

1. In order to lower your stress level, you will have to become a completely different person.   *True*   *False*

2. Practicing the skills in this book is one sure way to control your anxiety and stress.   *True*   *False*

3. Motivation is important, but not necessary in the treatment of stress.   *True*   *False*

4. Having other people in your life actively involved in your stress management program is one way to help you practice your skills.   *True*   *False*

5. An excellent form of self-control involves using both the help of others as well as material rewards.   *True*   *False*

Lesson 1 Exercise

6. Keeping formal records of your behavior in stressful situations should be done for at least two weeks.   *True*   *False*

7. It is often easy to overlook stress triggers in your life, which can make your stressful feelings increase.   *True*   *False*

8. Most emotional reactions are all-or-none events that happen with almost equal intensity.   *True*   *False*

9. The Daily Stress Record is meant to be used to record your major stressful events of each day.   *True*   *False*

10. Each time you experience an increase in your level of stress, you should note it on the Stressful Events Record.   *True*   *False*

11. The averages of the background stress level and highest stress level for each week should be graphed on the Progress Chart.   *True*   *False*

Lesson 2 Exercise

12. The parasympathetic nervous system protects the body by preventing intense emotions, like anxiety, to spiral to extremely high levels.   *True*   *False*

13. It is dangerous for your heart to beat too rapidly or forcefully while you are experiencing stress.   *True*   *False*

14. Even a little stress in your life can be detrimental to your health.   *True*   *False*

15. Stress is a natural reaction or response to possible threatening or challenging situations. It is the only logical response to these situations.   *True*   *False*

16. It is possible to vacillate between a state of stress and anxiety when responding to challenging situations.   *True*   *False*

17. The physical response system to stress may provide symptoms, such as increased heart rate, fast breathing, chest pains, and a choking sensation.   *True*   *False*

Lesson 3 Exercise

18. Learning relaxation techniques means learning how to reduce tension in all areas of your body at the same time.   *True*   *False*

19. Deep Muscle Relaxation involves isolating muscle tension, concentrating on the feeling it produces, and then flopping when tension is released.   *True*   *False*

20. It is important to focus on the word "relax" each time you breathe in during Deep Muscle Relaxation.   *True*   *False*

21. You should practice Deep Muscle Relaxation at least twice a day for 20 minutes each time.   *True*   *False*

Lesson 4 Exercise

22. Your emotions are caused and changed by your thoughts and beliefs about an event, not by the event itself.   *True*   *False*

23. Because the majority of your thoughts are automatic, it is impossible to control them.   *True*   *False*

24. The lower the realistic probability of an event, the greater will be the intensity of your emotion.   *True*   *False*

25. Realistically looking at all the evidence means seeing both the positive and negative aspects of a possible event. *True* *False*

26. The level of intensity in the last column of the Realistic Thinking Sheet will ideally be less than the level that had first been recorded. *True* *False*

Lesson 5 Exercise

27. A person who jumps to conclusions about an event with the worst possible outcome in mind is catastrophizing. *True* *False*

28. Realistic thinking is not the same as positive thinking. *True* *False*

29. The mind can cope with anything, including tragedies or catastrophes. *True* *False*

30. You should not try to be your own professional by examining your underlying thoughts and feelings. *True* *False*

Lesson 6 Exercise

31. The first of the three times you do discrimination training, you tense and relax to one-half of maximum before flopping. *True* *False*

32. Portability means being able to relax in shorter amounts of time by reducing the number of muscle groups tensed and relaxed. *True* *False*

33. While doing relaxation by recall, you tense and relax muscle groups while imagining the word "relax" every time you exhale. *True* *False*

34. It is best to generalize your relaxation skills gradually as you strengthen your concentration. *True* *False*

35. It is wrong to expect that you will be able to relax during stressful events all the time *True* *False*

36. After you get the hang of relaxation by recall and can do it in any situation, you don't need to practice it anymore. *True* *False*

Lesson 7 Exercise

37. One effective way to help you be more objective about the events in your life is to view a particular situation from someone else's vantage point. *True* *False*

38. Worrying about an event helps to lessen possible negative consequences of the event and is beneficial. *True* *False*

39. To properly do prediction testing, you must make highly specific guesses about the outcome of an event. *True* *False*

40. Creativity is a valuable tool when devising tests to check your predictions. *True* *False*

Lesson 8 Exercise

41. Because it is aimed at reversing your tendency to avoid or escape situations, reality testing focuses on the behavioral system. *True* *False*

42. You must stay in the stressful situation long enough for your stress level to decrease for reality testing to be accurate. *True* *False*

43. Doing reality testing because you have to, instead of because you want to, does not make much difference so long as it is done. *True* *False*

44. The situations that you indicate as stressful should be first on your stepladder. *True* *False*

Lesson 9 Exercise

45. You can accomplish more in a day if you overcommit yourself to too many tasks because you will do each faster. *True* *False*

46. To be assertive with your time is to limit unnecessary and unimportant activities and interruptions. *True* *False*

47. It is better to tackle tasks as each arises versus putting them off until a later time. *True* *False*

48. "B" tasks are important and are completed the same day. *True* *False*

49. You should first estimate the time required to finish a task and then double that time. *True* *False*

Lesson 10 Exercise

50. The first thing to do when facing a problem is to define it in specific details. *True* *False*

51. A common error encountered with facing a problem is the tendency to believe that there is no possible solution. *True* *False*

52. Brainstorming refers to the idea of thinking hard for a long time for one good idea to use as a solution to a problem.   *True*   *False*

53. It is not necessary to apply realistic thinking skills once you have brainstormed for solutions to a problem.   *True*   *False*

Lesson 11 Exercise

54. Being assertive is the act of voicing your rights and feelings to others appropriately and respectfully.   *True*   *False*

55. You do not really need your realistic thinking techniques while being assertive, for you will not have time to do them while trying to be assertive.   *True*   *False*

56. The difficulty for people in assertiveness training is in learning how to be assertive.   *True*   *False*

57. Assertive behavior does not generally reduce stress disorders, but it will make you feel better.   *True*   *False*

58. The stepladder of situations can be applied to situations in which you need to be assertive.   *True*   *False*

Afterword Exercise

59. The evidence is unclear whether or not certain prescribed drugs are effective for stress relief.   *True*   *False*

60. It is possible to become dependent upon benzodiazepines with prolonged use.   *True*   *False*

61. You will not experience withdrawal effects from going off prolonged use of benzodiazepines.   *True*   *False*

62. The more gradual and paced your withdrawal from medication, the better your chances of eliminating your dependency.   *True*   *False*

63. Although some people have mastered stress using the principles in this book while in the process of withdrawal from drugs, they still experience stress during withdrawal and find it very difficult to cope.   *True*   *False*

Answers to Self-Assessment Exercises

Introduction

1. ***False***   Changing your level of stress requires you to learn new ways of thinking about and reacting to stressful situations. While you will not become a different person after doing this, your life will be different - more enjoyable and satisfying.

2. ***True***   Even though the lessons and skills in this book can be learned by nearly everyone, they won't do much good unless they are regularly put into practice.

3. ***False***   It is important and necessary to be motivated in this program if you want the full benefits of reducing your stress. Self-control techniques help to keep you motivated when you are tempted not to do the exercises and assignments.

4. ***True***   Your family and friends can help you by being actively involved in your program and by supporting and encouraging your efforts.

5. ***True***   One good method to maintain your self-control is to enlist the aid of others while arranging material techniques to be applied. The more creative and appropriate ways you choose to do self-control techniques, the better.

Lesson 1

6. ***True***   For you to get a clear picture of your stress over a variety of situations and times, you need to keep formal records of your behaviors and thoughts for at least two weeks.

7. ***True***   It is not always the case that only major events trigger stress. The daily events of your life can add up and increase your stress without your awareness of it. This makes you feel out of control.

8. ***False***   Emotions are complex and vary in their intensity as will your stress level.

9. ***False***   Not only should you record any major stressful events in the Daily Stress Record, but also record the average level of stress and the highest level it reaches for each day.

10. ***True***   The Stressful Events Record can show you trends of your stress level; for example, it can give you an idea of the time, place, and situation in which you repeatedly feel an increase in stress.

11. ***True***   All the information you need for the Progress Chart comes from your Daily Stress Record. You just plot the averages of the background and highest levels of stress for each week on the chart and connect the points after each week.

Lesson 2

12. **True** While the sympathetic nervous system gets the body in gear and prepared for a fight/flight response, the parasympathetic nervous system restores the body to a more relaxed state. Because of this protective and automatic feature of the parasympathetic nervous system, anxiety levels cannot soar infinitely higher.

13. **False** An increased heart rate helps your tissues receive enough oxygen, and your muscles enough blood, to react quickly and powerfully to a threat or challenge. Although some uncomfortable symptoms, such as dizziness, sweating and muscle tension may occur, they are natural and harmless.

14. **False** A mild level of stress in appropriate situations (for example, before taking an exam) is a boost to your motivation, mental awareness and attention. Too high levels of stress, however, can interfere with your physical health and emotional well-being.

15. **False** Stress is a natural response to a threat or a challenge. However, it is not the only response to being in the situation. Excitement, depression and anxiety are also other responses you can experience. Which response you have depends upon your perceived ability to cope with the particular situation you are facing.

16. **True** Anxiety and stress are closely related. Most people who are highly stressed occasionally have bouts of anxiety, periods when they feel they are losing control.

17. **True** The physical responses to stress, increased heart rate, fast breathing, etc., are the body's way of preparing you for danger.

Lesson 3

18. **False** You only need to learn how to reduce tension in the body where tension is not needed at the moment.

19. **True** The idea behind this relaxation technique is to alternately tense and relax muscle groups. The goal is to acquire the ability to observe and to isolate tension in the body.

20. **False** Focus on the word "relax" when breathing out.

21. **True** Practicing the relaxation technique two or more times every day, 20 minutes each time, helps you to learn and use this skill more quickly and effectively.

Lesson 4

22. **True** Although many people believe that events are what cause stress, in fact, it is the thoughts which cause you to react emotionally to a situation.

23. **False** It is possible with practice to learn how to control all your thoughts and consequently your emotional reactions, no matter if they seem "automatic."

24. **False** An emotion's intensity will be less when its realistic probability is lower. To control your anxious thoughts, you should be striving to reach low estimates of realistic probability.

25. **True**   It is often the case that people bothered by anxious thoughts focus on the negative and bypass the positive.

26. **True**   Over time and with some realistic evidence and alternative consequences in mind, the emotional intensity level in the last column will ideally decrease from the level in the third column.

Lesson 5

27. **True**   A person who catastrophizes will automatically assume that an absolute tragedy will be the consequence of an event.

28. **True**   When a person thinks realistically about the likelihood of an event, he or she looks at the negative as well as positive outcomes. This process gives a more accurate estimate of an event's possible consequences.

29. **True**   While it is natural and often vital to have strong emotional reactions to serious events in one's life, it is a fact that the human mind is equipped to cope with even the direst tragedy.

30. **False**   In the Realistic Thinking Sheet, you pinpoint your "bottom line" of belief. The way to do this is to ask yourself "what if" after a consequence and repeat this until you arrive at the underlying basic thought. Remember to talk to yourself.

Lesson 6

31. **False**   The first time involves tensing and relaxing each muscle group about three-quarters of your maximum before flopping, the second time, about half your maximum, and the third, about a quarter of your maximum.

32. **True**   The idea behind portability is to make relaxation possible in a variety of different situations and times throughout the day.

33. **False**   No muscle groups are tensed during relaxation by recall. Instead, the focus is on smoothly breathing as you say "in" when inhaling and "relax" when exhaling.

34. **True**   Just as an athlete can strain muscles without a warm-up or without the skills necessary in a certain competition, you should avoid feelings of frustration and failure by gradually increasing the difficulty of relaxation.

35. **True**   Situations and times vary, so sometimes it will be more difficult to relax. With practice, you improve your ability to relax anytime and anywhere.

36. **False**   Aside from its ease and quick application, relaxation by recall should not be difficult to practice two or three times each week for maximum effectiveness.

Lesson 7

37. **True**   By looking at your situation as an observer rather than as a participant (or even a victim), you can be more objective and realistic about it.

38. **False**   The "magic of worry," the tendency to excessively worry about an event with the hope of changing its outcome, is a myth that only serves to make the worrier miserable.

39. **True**   Vague guesses about an event's consequences will not give good indications of your predictions.

40. *True* It can be a challenge at times to test your predictions, so imagination and creativity are great assets in devising precise and valid tests.

Lesson 8

41. *True* Reality testing is a method to get you to expose yourself to stressful situations in your life. In this sense, it works on your behaviors.

42. *True* When you escape from or avoid situations, your stress level tends to increase.

43. *False* When you do something you want to, you perform the task more systematically. This makes you feel more in control and, therefore, less anxious.

44. *False* Reality testing will not work well if you attempt very difficult tasks at first.

Lesson 9

45. *False* The only thing overcommitment does is to make you feel anxious and overwhelmed. Chances are, you will not perform at your peak because of lost time worrying about all you have to get done.

46. *True* Assertiveness goes a long way in helping you be more efficient with your tasks and less overwhelmed with interfering tasks or interruptions.

47. *False* You need to learn how to concentrate on one task at a time, even if other tasks arise as a result of the task. Doing too many tasks at once does not allow you to stick to an agenda, which is an essential step in time management.

48. *False* "B" tasks are important. However, they don't necessarily have to be done the same day.

49. *True* With unexpected setbacks or interruptions, tasks can take longer than predicted. It is wise to give yourself extra time to finish a task.

Lesson 10

50. *True* People usually conceptualize their problems in global ways. That is, they define their problems in broad and vague terms. This serves to make problems "overwhelming" and "uncontrollable."

51. *True* It is rare that a problem cannot be solved, although it is common that solutions are hard to find.

52. *False* What brainstorming really does is help you think of a number of possible solutions in order to pick the best one.

53. *False* A solution is only as good as its ability to solve a problem. After you brainstorm for possible solutions, you have to assess the effectiveness of particular solutions and identify the best solution from your list.

Lesson 11

54. *True* The importance of appropriateness in being assertive is undeniable. To stand up for your rights does not mean to trample those in your way.

55. *False*   You should always use your realistic thinking techniques. With practice, you will be able to evaluate the pros and cons of a situation quickly and thoroughly, until assertiveness becomes almost automatic.

56. *False*   Usually people have more trouble accepting and feeling comfortable with their assertive behavior.

57. *False*   Not only will assertive behavior reduce stress, but it will also increase your sense of control and, hence, enhance your ability to cope with stressful events.

58. *True*   The stepladder together with realistic thinking skills can greatly help your assertiveness training.

Afterword

59. *False*   There is strong evidence that certain drugs are effective, at least for a short time, in reducing stress in some people.

60. *True*   One tends to develop a tolerance to the benzodiazepines which would require an increase in dosage to maintain effectiveness; this makes one vulnerable to developing a dependency on the drug.

61. *False*   You will have stress symptoms reoccur after you stop taking a benzodiazepine. It is critical to be under a physician's care and advice while on these drugs.

62. *True*   The relapse rates for coming off the benzodiazepines, for example, are high. A slow and steady schedule of withdrawal as set by your physician is the safest course.

63. *False*   Most people who apply the learning principles to stressful situations do not find the reemergence of stress during withdrawal a problem. They have learned how to accept, cope with, and master their stress.

the LEARN education center

The LEARN Education Center was established to respond to the increasing demand for scientifically sound, state-of-the-art publications, training courses and services. The Center is dedicated to the continuing development of health and wellness materials, including audio tapes, newsletters, professional training guides, leadership training programs, and professional counseling services.

Publications currently available from The LEARN Education Center are as follows:

The LEARN Program for Weight Control by Kelly D. Brownell, Ph.D.

The LEARN Program Monitoring Forms

The LEARN Program Cassettes by Kelly D. Brownell, Ph.D.

Making a Weight Loss Program Work - The LEARN Program Leaders Guide by Kelly D. Brownell, Ph.D.

The Weight Maintenance Survival Guide by Kelly D. Brownell, Ph.D. and Judith Rodin, Ph.D.

The Personal Maintenance Kit by Kelly D. Brownell, Ph.D. and Judith Rodin, Ph.D.

The Weight Control Digest - Professional Edition

The Weight Control Digest - Consumer Edition

Living With Exercise by Steven N. Blair, P.E.D.

Mastering Stress - A LifeStyle Approach by David H. Barlow, Ph.D. and Ronald M. Rapee, Ph.D.

ordering information

This manual and the other materials distributed through The LEARN Education Center are not available in bookstores. You may write or call the number listed below to obtain current pricing and shipping charges. Discounts are available for bulk orders.

For your ordering convenience, a toll free number is available and may be called 24 hours a day. Payments can be made with your MasterCard, VISA or by mailing your personal check. You may also fax a copy of your purchase order. All orders are shipped within 24 hours of receipt, and next day and second day delivery service is available. As you use our publications, we sincerely welcome any comments you may have that would make these materials even better, and we encourage you to tell us how we are doing.

For ordering or general information, please write or call us at:

The LEARN Education Center
1555 W. Mockingbird Lane, Suite 203
Dallas, Texas 75235

Our toll free number is (800) 736-7323
In Dallas (214) 637-7700
Our fax number is (214) 637-0529